ENDORS

It is with a real excitement that I recommend the reading of this wonderful book. Oftentimes people speak on a subject to which there is little familiarity; here is a testimony of the work of grace in the heart of a man. Bill Stafford III had become a trophy of grace. God in His mercy, grace and forgiveness has radically changed this man's heart. How encouraging it is when we can read the story of one that can encourage us to draw our strength from a source that is unlimited. I believe that you will be overwhelmed as you hear the story from Bill Stafford III, as well as his father, in the work that was literally observed as it was taking place in the deep recesses of the heart. I commend this book for the reading of encouragement to God's faithfulness. You will be blessed.

Dr. Johnny Hunt, Pastor
First Baptist Woodstock
Woodstock, GA

Bill Stafford III, has written a story which every pastor, pastor's wife and pastor's child needs to read. His story is deeply moving. It is also a story that should serve as a word of warning and encouragement for all of us in the ministry.

Jerry Vines, Pastor
First Baptist Church
Jacksonville, FL

ENDORSEMENTS

The testimony of Bill Stafford III is a testimony of the grace of God. Of course, for all of us that is true, but in some cases the marvel of God's grace constitutes an incredible encouragement to those who at some point have stumbled or fallen. For all of us then Bill Stafford's story is one that will warm your heart, encourage your spirit, and give you the courage to plow on. God bless Bill Stafford III and everyone who reads this book.

Paige Patterson, President
Southeastern Baptist Theological Seminary
Wake Forest, NC

H Not Beyond OPE

A Pastor and His Prodigal Son

BY
BILL STAFFORD III WITH VICTOR MAXWELL

INTRODUCTION BY ADRIAN ROGERS

AMBASSADOR-EMERALD INTERNATIONAL
GREENVILLE, SOUTH CAROLINA • BELFAST, NORTHERN IRELAND

Not Beyond Hope:
A Pastor and His Prodigal Son

Copyright © 2000 Bill Stafford III

All Rights Reserved
No part of this book may be reproduced, stored in a retrieval system,
or transmitted in any form or by any means—electronic, mechanical,
photocopy, recording, or otherwise—without written permission of
the publisher, except for brief quotation in written reviews.

ISBN: 1-889893-60-9

Published by:
Ambassador-Emerald International
427 Wade Hampton Blvd.
Greenville, SC 29609 USA

and

Ambassador Productions
Ardenlee Street
Belfast, Northern Ireland
BT6 8QJ

www.emeraldhouse.com

Cover and internal design by Brad Sherman
Cover design © 2000 Grand Design

CONTENTS

INTRODUCTION

I believe in miracles because I believe in God. We serve the God Who can open blind eyes, straighten crooked limbs, and even raise the dead. There is nothing too hard for Him. Ours is a supernatural faith and our God is the mighty God.

Having said that, I am firmly convinced that the miracles of grace are even greater than the miracles of glory. Jesus displayed His glory when he turned water into sparkling wine, but He demonstrated His grace when He transformed Bill Stafford from a devilish derelict and made him a monument to mercy.

Why are miracles of grace the greater miracles? Because they come at a far greater price. When Jesus made the universe, He did it by the Word of His power. He spoke and stars dripped from His fingers. But when He redeems and justifies a sinner, it takes more than a word. The awful price for sin had to be paid in order for God to be both just and the justifier of those that believe. That price was the agony and blood of an old rugged cross. It took the silver of Jesus' tears and the gold of His blood to ransom sinners like we are. Jesus baptized His very soul in hell to redeem the race. That, friend, is why the story that you will read is such a miracle.

Bill Stafford was a young man hell bent. He had been taken captive by the unholy trinity - the world, the flesh and the devil. His life story was written with the ink of rebellion on the tablet of a hard heart. Sure there were some times when he tried to do better, but without God, man's best is not enough.

But there is the other side and the rest of the story. Young Bill was soaked in prayer by loving and heartbroken parents. As a result of prayer that would not take no for an answer, Bill Stafford was arrested by the loving Hand of God and taken captive to grace. Formerly a slave to his flesh and to Satan himself, he has now been made a servant to the Lord Jesus Christ.

This story is a true one that should bless and warm the hearts of thousands. It will be an encouragement to parents who may be tempted to lose heart and cease to pray for a wayward child. It will be a word of motivation to never cease sharing the Gospel of Jesus Christ, which is indeed the power of God unto salvation.

I trust that the reader will be impressed to pray for the ministry of Bill Stafford, and I pray that this volume will have wide distribution and a life changing effect on all who read it.

Adrian Rogers, Pastor
Bellevue Baptist Church

CHAPTER I
TOUGH LOVE

Young Bill Stafford turned his silver Grand Prix automobile into the narrow lane that led to his parents' farmhouse. Quietly he drove up the slight incline. The pale moon lit up the rolling hills surrounding the ranch style house, which occupied an elevated yet, secluded site above the eighty-eight acre farm. The Staffords lived in an isolated region of Bradley County, about thirty miles out of Chattanooga, Tennessee.

It was three o'clock in the morning. Bill had almost perfected the art of sneaking up the half-mile gravel track to the final approach at the side of the house without disturbing his parents. He had done this many times before. Slowly he edged the car past his sister's mobile home near his dad's red barns. Bill winced at the noise of the gravel crunching under the rolling tires. There were no lights on in the mobile home so he knew that Brenda and her family were all sleeping. He was also sure his parents would have retired to bed hours earlier.

For Bill it had been another great night out with his teenage friends. He had had a blast, and he did not want to spoil the night of fun with an unnecessary confrontation with his preacher father. In spite of the fine role model given by his godly parents, Dr. & Mrs. Bill Stafford, young Bill persisted in doing his own thing. He was nineteen years old, and like most of the youth of his generation Bill preferred to follow his peers and be popular with his friends rather than walk in the footsteps of his Christian parents.

He was aware that he had been leading a double life. At home he acted the part of a Christian and was active in the church program. However, for four years he had tried to hide from his parents his accelerating indulgence in drugs and increasing addiction to narcotics. Furthermore, he needed more money to finance his growing habit than the few dollars he earned at Baskin Robins. This had forced Bill to turn to petty thieving. He stole from his Mom's purse. Her silence on the matter made Bill conclude she had not missed the money.

Carefully he steered the automobile to the side of the building, and as quietly as possible he eased himself out of the vehicle. Stepping on to the back porch he was wary not to kick over any pots or plant boxes. As he passed a window near the door Bill was startled to see a light still burning in the family room. At first he thought his mother must still be awake.

Slowly he pulled the storm door open hoping not to make too much noise. Just as he unlocked and opened the kitchen door he recognized the shadowy profile of someone sitting in the reclining chair. It was not his mother as he had first thought. He was startled to discover it was his father. Bill instinctively knew something was wrong. In that split second he broke into a cold sweat, and alarm bells seemed to begin ringing in his head. He felt guilty and almost wanted to step outside again. He feared his deepening indulgence in soft and hard drugs had finally caught up with him and knew in his heart that his dad must have become aware of his growing obsession with narcotics.

The opening of the kitchen door startled his dad. He had been dozing on the comfortable recliner for a few hours waiting for this moment to confront his wayward son. Bill and Sue Stafford's anxiety for Bill had not only caused them deep searching of their hearts, it had finally brought them to a crisis in which they had to make a very tough decision. They had talked for a long time earlier the previous evening and both of them wept as they earnestly prayed for young Bill. It had broken their hearts to discover that the son, for whom they prayed daily and for whom they had high hopes, was trafficking drugs and bringing narcotics into their home.

Days previously Dr. Stafford had happened to be looking for something in Bill's car when he found a small bag. He afterwards learned it was marijuana. He refused to return the bags to his son, and as a result Bill lost a considerable sum of money. The marijuana had been bought by Bill and was to be passed on to his friends. His parents had also found small empty bags in Bill's room. This led them to conclude that their son was also hooked on drugs. The climax came when Bill's mom discovered that Bill had been raiding her purse, and some of her money was missing.

The Staffords were commitment to maintaining a consistent Christian testimony in their home, and at this time they had a twelve-year-old son, Bill's brother Steven, and were fearful of the possible influence drugs might have on him. They were aware that narcotics could also jeopardize Bill's life and future, and they decided they would finally have to take some strong action to try and rescue their teenage boy from his self-destructive behavior. Mom and Dad had given Bill so many warnings in the past and had vainly tried to curb his willful lifestyle. Now the time had arrived; Dr. Stafford braced himself.

"Hi Dad," said Bill as he looked at the tall slender figure of his Dad in the glow of the soft light.

Dr. Stafford did not take any time for pleasantries or preliminaries. "Bill, this is the final straw." His tone was sober and serious. "Your mom and I can't take any more of your persistent indulgence in drugs, and now we find you have been stealing from your mom's purse. We have given you every opportunity Bill and have tried to correct and warn you too many times. It is tough for me to say this son, but you have two weeks either to straighten up or move out."

"That's fine with me Dad," retorted Bill even though he was initially stunned at the thought of the unexpected ultimatum. He had never been separated from his family before. Although his father was a genial and compassionate man, Bill knew he was also a strong disciplinarian. When his dad said something like this, young Bill knew that he meant it.

An awkward, embarrassing silence followed Bill's reply. He could not think of anything else to say. Half-heartedly Bill bade his father goodnight and made his way to his bedroom. His dad put out the lights before retiring to his room with a heavy heart.

Bill lay on top of the bed unable to sleep, partly due to being high on dope but also still reeling from his father's ultimatum. He had already been planning to move out, but his father had beaten him to it and pre-empted Bill's decision.

He remembered the recent Saturday night party he had thrown for his friends at the farmhouse while his mom and dad were away conducting revival meetings. Bill had defied the strict principles of his Christian home and had provided an abundance of alcohol and drugs for the evening. He and his friends partied until the small hours of Sunday morning as heavy smoke hung in the still summer air and heavy metal music smashed the silence of the what was normally a quiet countryside farm. Because the holding was in an isolated area there was no danger of disturbing any neighbors.

Around midnight some of the kids went home but others opted to stay all night. The next morning it seemed there were young people lying everywhere. Beer cans and liquor bottles littered the yard and floated in the swimming pool at the front of the house. After the friends finally left in the afternoon Bill cleaned the house as best he could knowing that his parents were returning a few days later.

On their return Bill's mom and dad had learned of the drunken spree during their absence. There was some straight talking from father to son on that occasion, but it had made little difference to Bill. Dr. Stafford was never embarrassed in telling his children how much they were loved. However, he felt that there were times when love must be tough. As a result Bill was not trusted to be at home alone again. Although Bill respected his mom and dad, he was also rebellious and refused to modify his behavior.

Bill reasoned the whole episode over in his mind as he lay on his bed. "Two weeks to straighten up or get out. Ugh! I've never cussed nor insulted them, and yet they tell me to straighten up? Why should I? I've already tried to do that and I was miserable. I'm enjoying my life. Being a preacher's kid is not my idea of living. Why couldn't I have been born in a normal home?

Perhaps my best plan is to move out. I have always wanted to be on my own so that I didn't have to go to church and be religious. At least when I move out I will be free to do whatever I want. There will be no more restraints or carping. I'll do my own thing. I'll show Mom and Dad that I can make it on my own."

Eventually Bill drifted into unconsciousness.

The bright sunlight streaming through the window wakened Bill from his shallow sleep just after dawn. He had been asleep for only a few hours. The singing of the birds in trees around the house did not change his somber mood nor distract him from the same predicament that had dominated his mind when he drifted off to sleep. "There is definitely no way I am staying. No sir, I have too many restraints on my life here at home, and I have too much to lose."

Bill lay on his bed wide-awake debating in his mind what his next move should be. "Where can I go? I know John's folks will give me a place to stay. I've stayed there many times, and I even spoke to John about moving out of here. They will give me a bed, and then I'll get myself a job."

Eventually Bill made his way into the kitchen to eat some breakfast. Dad was already at the table and his mother was busy fixing some coffee. The atmosphere was uncomfortable and somewhat tense. Bill knew his folks were upset, but there was no point in prolonging the pain. Obviously their minds were made up and so was Bill's. Hardly a word was spoken between them until Bill finally announced in a coarse voice, "I'm moving out later today." He could say no more as he choked up to hold back his tears.

The words seared his mom's heart and were as sharp as a sword to his dad's soul. Dr. and Mrs. Stafford felt there was little more they could say. Tears coursed down their faces. "Where are you going to live?" his dad asked.

"I'm going to John's house." Bill responded. His parents knew that Bill and John had been best friends for several years, but for some time they had been suspicious that both boys shared the same fascination for drugs and girls. Girls were fine but not drugs. They feared these teenage boys were on the slippery slopes that could land them in trouble.

"Bill, we love you and are praying for you, but if you don't change, you are going to ruin your life," his mother pleaded.

It seemed as if her words fell on deaf ears. Bill never answered. Tears continued to stream down their faces. A lump came to Bill's throat, but he was too embarrassed to cry so he walked out of the kitchen and returned to his bedroom.

From the phone in his bedroom Bill called his best friend, John, and told him that he was leaving home. He outlined the circumstances that led to the sudden decision and then asked if he could take his things over to John's house for a few days. The two guys arranged to meet in the parking lot of the Mount Vernon Baptist Church.

Bill's thoughts towards his parents were paradoxical. On one hand he was angry and resentful, yet in his heart he was elated. He was sad to be leaving home, yet he was glad he would be free to do what he wanted.

After breakfast Bill crammed his clothes and other personal effects into a case. It all seemed so unreal that he was packing to leave home. He was not going off to camp or for a visit to his relatives. This was it. He was moving out. For some time he had had a chip on his shoulder about being a preacher's kid. Now he could hardly believe he was being evicted from his own house while his father was still a preacher. It even seemed more bizarre when his mom and dad helped him load his baggage into the trunk of his car.

In a clumsy way Bill bade his parents good bye. Mrs. Stafford kissed her son on the cheek and asked, "When will we see you again?"

"I'll call soon," Bill answered. This was no time to arrange dates or promise visits.

Dad hugged Bill tightly and assured him, "Son, we are always here for you. We love you and will be praying for you."

Bill found it hard to fight back the tears. Once released from his Dad's hug he climbed into his car, turned the ignition key and the engine roared into life. He slipped the car into gear and accelerated down the same driveway he had sneaked up very early that morning. He was aware he was turning his back on his family, on the beautiful home with its large swimming pool and on the farm with its outbuildings and the beautiful green pasture where cattle and horses grazed lazily. He tried to put it all out of his mind and drove towards the main highway.

Dr. and Mrs. Stafford stood in the driveway of their home and watched as Bill's car sped down the lane kicking up clouds of dust in its wake. When the car disappeared from view mom and dad hugged each other and wept on each other's shoulders. They did not retire until very late that night, but even when they did there was no sleep for either during the long hours until dawn.

For almost thirty miles Bill sped along the winding roads towards the Mount Vernon Church. The crisp air rushed through the open windows of his car. It seemed as if the feelings of sadness and blues were being carried off on the wings of the wind. He began to savor his first taste of freedom and release from the restraints of home. He felt as though he were as free as a bird escaped from a cage. Although he had turned his back on home, he knew he was finally clear of all the restrictions and expectations that had hindered his enjoyment of youth as a preacher's kid.

Driving through the Tennessee country roads towards his planned rendezvous with John, young Bill Stafford, although carefree in spirit, was unaware that the road he had chosen was not only a windy one, it was downhill in more ways than one.

CHAPTER 2
HOME SWEET HOME

The Stafford's home in the Rivermont district of Chattanooga was a small three-bedroom parsonage located next door to the church. The house was always a hive of activity. Dr. Bill Stafford was a very successful, well known preacher and pastor of the growing Lupton Drive Baptist Church in the city. Besides the busy pastorate he was also much in demand as an evangelist and conference speaker which necessitated frequent trips to churches in other states.

Mrs. Stafford did not enjoy good health when her five children were growing up. Her husband's frequent preaching trips away from home plus his hardworking and busy pastorate brought added strains and stresses to raising five kids on the doorstep of the church.

Bobby was the oldest of the Stafford children, and he was followed by Brenda and Karen. Bill was seven years younger than brother Bobby and seven years older than the Stafford's youngest son, Steven. The age difference between the boys did not allow them to forge as close a bond as that which existed between sisters Brenda and Karen.

The five Stafford kids created a lot of fun and noise around the house. Like other children of their age they had their rough and tumble days which resulted in grazed knees, cut fingers and chewing gum stuck in their hair. Other children from the neighbourhood and some from the church sometimes joined them to play in their yard which at times was transformed into a playground.

Due to Mrs. Stafford's recurrent illnesses it was necessary to hire someone to help with the daily chores. Friends at the church recommended Margaret, a Christian lady unknown to the family but who soon became a very close friend. Margaret was employed to care for the five boisterous children. There was

plenty of work for her to do. Besides cleaning, cooking and looking after the kids, Margaret also made sure that all five young
Staffords did not miss church or be late for their classes at the
nearby Rivermont Elementary School.

Being preacher's kids, the Stafford children were expected
to follow a strict code of behavior both at home and in the
church. Mom and Dad Stafford tried to invest love and affection
in their children and deposit proper values into their lives. In
doing so, certain things were inevitably made off limits. No
worldly music was permitted in the house. All comics and magazines needed to contain wholesome reading. These rules were
not set up as spoilsports of the children's fun but as roadblocks
on life's highway to try to protect the Stafford kids from the hazards and disasters that might lurk up ahead.

Even when dad was away preaching, all five Stafford children were expected to be present at church every Sunday. To
young Bill it seemed as though the church program was an
extension of their family life and the church building was their
second home. The Stafford kids were scrupulously required to
follow the Sunday School program. They sang in all the different choirs and attended the various church camps.

These disciplines frequently left a durable impression on
young Bill's mind. There were times he rebelled against rules in the
home, and his dad left a different sort of impression on the more
tender parts of young Bill's anatomy. He recalls one such incident,

> I was sitting in the back of the church talking
> with my friends one Sunday evening. Suddenly, in the
> middle of the service I noticed that my dad had left the
> platform and was walking straight toward me. Dad did
> not tolerate any of us talking in church, and if he
> caught us he would either call us down to the front of
> the church where he could watch us, or if we were real-
> ly bad, he would come and get us. I must have been
> really bad for I knew he was coming to get me. When

dad called you down, we kids were in big trouble, but when he came after me, then I knew I was dead!

He walked all the way to the back of the church to where we sat. Dad ignored the other boys but took a firm hold of my shoulder and virtually dragged me right down the aisle to the front pew where he plumped me down. He told me he could watch me better at the front. The whole church had seen what had happened, and I was so embarrassed. I knew I was a goner when I got home, so I fervently prayed that one of two things would happen—either revival would come down from heaven and get dad so busy with the things of the Lord that he might forget about me, or I would pray, "Lord since you are coming back anyway, could you please do it now?" Unfortunately, neither happened, and I got my just reward when I got home.

Because Bill was frequently paraded to the front pew at Lupton Drive Church, he had full view of the activities at the "mourner's bench." He still has vivid memories of people coming forward at invitation time every Sunday and kneeling at that old bench. The young boy could never understand why there were puddles of tears where the people silently sobbed and prayed. His dad would often join them at the front and weep with them. He did not realize that those tears were spilled for Bill and his brothers and sisters. It was not until years later that Bill appreciated that those people were sincere and must have been in touch with God.

When dad was at home he got so deeply engrossed in church work, and at times was under such great pressures, that his children found it difficult to understand why daddy was always busy. The kids wanted to spend time with their dad just like other families, but he seemed to be engrossed in church work all the time. They concluded that the stresses and strains which were piled on the pastor and which robbed them of his attention were normal for a preacher.

In recollection Dr. Stafford regrets that his family's interests were sacrificed to a mistaken order of priorities he had adopted as a zealous Independent Baptist preacher. Dr. Stafford attributes this mistake to his distorted and erroneous view of the ministry.

> My philosophy of ministry was fundamentally flawed. I thought that busyness was equal to blessing and God was pleased with the amount of work I did. The busier I was the more blessing I expected. Undoubtedly God had first place in my life, but after God the church came second, outside ministry was third, and then came the family in whatever time I had left. That was wrong but I didn't see it that way.

At times Pastor Stafford tried to make up for his absence from home by either taking Bill with him on a preaching trip or taking the family on vacation to a Bible camp. Young Bill remembers meeting other preachers' kids at the Milldale Bible Camp, near Zachary, Louisiana. Dr. Stafford and Dr. Manley Beasley preached at the camp every year so their families became close, and young Bill became friendly with Dr. Beasley's son. The two boys had a lot in common and took full advantage of a week away from the parsonage. Bill also remembers one real happy vacation when Dad took the family to visit Bill's aunts in far-off California. While there they were able to visit the shore for the first time in their lives.

When Dad was at home he sometimes took Bill to play T Ball. Eventually young Bill was able to gain a place on a Little League baseball team . Dressed in green and white colors Bill developed his skills as a catcher. His success on the playing field made him popular with other kids at school. However, he was not always so popular with Mrs. Allen, his teacher. Bill much preferred the wide open spaces and his sports activities to reading, writing and arithmetic in the dull confines of the classroom.

Like most growing boys, at times Bill seemed to have the appetite of a horse, the energy of a steam engine and the physical strength of a gorilla. His popularity grew amongst his school friends when he got to play quarterback on the flag football team while he was still only in fourth grade at the Rivermont Elementary School. He enjoyed the running, throwing and catching the ball and trying to evade tackles during the coaching sessions after school.

From as early as he could remember Bill hated being a preacher's kid and felt he was constantly living like a fish in a glass bowl. Because the Stafford family lived next to the church Bill resented the fact that everybody seemed to know all their family business. It seemed to young Bill that the church people were constantly coming by the house with their gripes and complaints. Even more annoying were the neighbours and church folk who seemed to single out the preacher's kids for any and every reason. These people were quick to tell Bill's parents how naughty he and his brothers and sisters had been. These complaints often got the Stafford kids into trouble with the pastor— their dad whom they thought was an overly zealous disciplinarian. What really made the Stafford children angry was that the same people who complained about them had their own kids who were far more mischievous and unruly than the pastor's children. It appeared these other kids escaped any sort of punishment because they were not the preacher's kids.

On some days Bill was left alone at home; he missed his brothers and friends. However, such days were also ideal for practicing his bat swing. Young Bill took his baseball bat and played an imaginary game at the back of the parsonage. He began to hit rocks toward the church as if he were playing in a big baseball game. He considered a rock hit over the church building as a home run. Sometimes the stones did not rise above the church roof but accidentally smashed through a window.

When dad returned home from his trips he strolled around the church, and when he saw the broken glass he could be heard muttering out loud to himself, "Who is it that keeps smashing these windows?"

With a straight face young Bill lied and told his Dad that it was probably someone messing around and throwing stones from the woods behind the house. Dad never did find out that the damage was due to the poor batting swing of his own son Bill.

The steep wooded hill behind the Stafford's house led up to a railroad track. When the train came through that part of the track their whole house shook as if an earthquake had visited Chattanooga. One day Bobby, Bill's oldest brother, and he climbed up to the top of the hill to the side of the rail track. They dug a deep foxhole in the soft red earth, and from their hidden vantage point they threw stones at the trains as they quickly hurled by. Even in such an isolated and wooded area the boys were spotted and reported for throwing stones. Again they got into trouble with their dad.

There were also many good times at Lupton Drive Baptist Church. Young Bill often spent weekends, or even vacation weeks, at the home of church members so he could play with their children. He especially enjoyed going to Granny Simms' home. Mr. & Mrs. Simms had only one son, and when Bill went to stay there they spoiled both boys. Bill so enjoyed Granny Simms' good home cooking that he still imagines he can still smell her home baked apple pies.

When Dr. Bill Stafford had been pastor of the Lupton Drive Baptist Church for over eleven years, he faced a major crisis. During those eleven years he had led the church through four building programs to accommodate a congregation that had rapidly grown from sixty souls to over one thousand attending on Sundays. However, the pressure of trying to maintain the busy and growing pastorate, attend to the many invitations to conduct revivals and care for his family began to take a heavy toll on Pastor Stafford. Furthermore, living in close proximity to the church only added to the mounting pressures and meant that there was little or no respite from the constant flow of people stopping by at their home.

At first Dr. Stafford thought he could handle the pressure. He was young and hard working, and he considered stress to be one of the hazards of being a pastor. However, as the pressures and demands increased, it became almost unbearable even for this hard working pastor to continue. He became so tense that on one occasion he had to disconnect all the phone lines in his house and draw all the curtains. He sat in the darkened isolation of his home and felt he could not face any more intrusions on his life.

Pastor Stafford was admitted to the hospital with nervous exhaustion and was told by the doctors that he would never preach again. In the hospital he was heavily sedated and put in an isolation unit to help him recover from his distress and trauma.

Dr. Stafford later admitted that this was the Lord's way of "bottoming" him out. He recalls,

> I told my wife I was finished. I'll give up the ministry and go and farm or get a job. I wanted to get away from it all. However, I found that when I threw in the towel God threw it right back at me. I could not free myself from His calling on my life.
>
> It was then that the Holy Spirit confronted me and transformed my life and ministry. Until then I had been depending on my own human resources to do God's work. That is why I became exhausted. It was only after I got to the end of my own resources that I discovered God did not expect me to do His work in my own strength, nor could I. It is God who does His work and gives the servant the energy and power to serve Him. At that point God challenged me to fully surrender my whole life to the will of God.

After this experience Dr. Stafford returned as senior pastor to Lupton Drive Baptist Church for two years. Even though the church was being blessed and experienced continued growth,

God challenged Dr. Stafford to leave the church and launch out into full time evangelism and conference ministry. It was a big step of faith.

The announcement of Pastor Bill Stafford's resignation from the pastorate shocked the people at Lupton Drive Baptist Church. It also stunned the wider Christian community and was front-page and headline news in the *Chattanooga News Free Press*, which was the most popular daily newspaper in the city.

This change of ministry meant that the Stafford family relocated to the leafy Northwood subdivision of Chattanooga. This transition also corresponded with Bill's transfer from Rivermont Elementary School to the Redbank Junior High School. However, due to the move, nine weeks later he had to transfer schools again to the Hixson Junior School.

These big adjustments for a young boy were not helped by Dr. Stafford being even more frequently absent from home than before when he was a pastor. Although the Stafford children did not fully appreciate what this meant at the time, Dad's absence began to build discontentment and bitterness in young Bill's heart. He felt he had even more reason than before to resent being looked upon as a preacher's kid.

Bill's bitter reaction at being singled out for trouble at home and at church motivated him to exert his physical strength among his peers at school. Even though he was a pre-teenager he had developed bodily strength beyond his years. It soon became clear that he had potential on the sports field. While he was at Hixson Junior High School the sports coach discovered that young Bill Stafford was a good all-rounder at football, baseball, basketball and track. Proudly, young Bill wore the black and gold colors of the Hixson Wildcats. He soon moved positions from halfback to middle-line-backer on the football field.

These sports activities gave Bill considerable satisfaction just to know that he was recognized and looked up to by other kids on the sports field. He felt he did not have to be a prudish preacher's son when he got involved in the rough and tumble of football or the fast pace of basketball. However, in spite of his athletic career beginning to flourish, Bill also became exposed to other pressures which ran contrary to the values he had been taught at home and against those practices which produced the best physical fitness he needed to be a sports star.

At twelve years old young Bill Stafford was on the threshold of what are sometimes known as the "tween years" – the time span between childhood and adulthood. During these years a young man's body clock seems to tick a little faster and bells begin to ring to awaken dormant hormones which soon begin to race through the boy's body. Monumental changes take place in the "tweenager's" social, physical, intellectual and moral world. The development of a boy's intellectual and moral capacity can largely be shaped and molded according to the environment and influences that are brought upon the adolescent.

It was at this impressionable age that Bill and some of his school friends, many of them from fine homes, were introduced to temptations that were to greatly influence their lives for years to come. It is sometimes difficult to know from where the first influences of adolescent perversion come. Until this point Bill had enjoyed a relatively sheltered family life in the parsonage. He had not yet been exposed to many of the pernicious elements of society. Perhaps Bill's decline was partly due to the normal youthful struggle to discover his own identity or even wrestling to find freedom from the imposed restrictions that he felt had been unfairly put upon him.

Whatever it might have been, while still at Rivermont School and even while his Dad was still pastoring Lupton Drive Baptist Church, Bill unwittingly got sucked into a group of school friends who started to experiment in smoking cigarettes and indulging in adult pornography. This inevitably led to more daring and sinister experiments which eventually led to enslaving vices and obsessions. Together these juveniles met in secret locations such as the basement of a house when parents were absent. They shared Playboy magazines, used language that Bill had never heard in his parents' home and smoked until some of them turned almost green with nausea.

Young Bill Stafford was deceived into thinking that these were the cool things to do. He could not have been more wrong.

CHAPTER 3
SPEED AND SPORTS

Building blocks are always among a boy's earliest toys. Dads often enjoy encouraging their children's intelligence by helping them build a house with the colored blocks. After the model house is completed and the last block has been put in place, one swipe from the child's hand can reduce the shaky construction to the original chaos of tumbled blocks scattered across the floor. Both father and son then have to start all over again on a new structure using the same blocks. The child will probably learn something of his ability to destroy, but it is the father who learns some lessons about building.

Many Christian parents try to lay the foundational building blocks of child raising in love, respect, honesty and all the virtues that accompany godliness. They are aware that their little children are as impressionable as wet cement which can be easily shaped and molded. However, the same parents can be heartbroken to see their children dismantle all those fundamental values with a youthful swipe of rebellion. At such a time it seems that their lives and hopes for their offspring lie in pieces. It is then that the parents need to return to the lessons learned from a child's building blocks. That parent needs a lot of patience to see the young life reconstructed out of the chaos of a misspent youth.

Just as Bill Stafford emerged into his teenage years he got entangled in the web of teenage revolution which was spreading like a prairie fire throughout the United States in the seventies. The Vietnam War was over, reactionary groups flourished, liberalism prevailed, and revolt against family values and authority became fashionable. Children and teenagers were most vulnerable as a wave of permissiveness swept through the American school system. Bill Stafford became a victim of this surge of permissiveness while in high school.

His continued passion for competitive and physical games initially made him a sports fanatic. He did not much care for the academic work of the classroom, but once he had donned the school's colors he felt a rush of exhilaration and action. Through his three years of junior high Bill developed his sporting talents in various disciplines. In early fall he was a middle linebacker for the Hixson Junior football team. During winter he was a sub-forward for the basketball squad and from early spring through to the summer he contributed to track and athletic events.

When Bill was a sophomore he was engaged in a period of intense training for a coming track meet. The school track coach observed some potential in the agile newcomer and soon discovered that Bill had good long jumping ability. The young guy was able to jump ninety-nine inches from a standing position. The coach said to him, "Hi kid, have you ever long-jumped?"

After Bill answered in the negative the coach said, "If you are able to do this from a standing position, it will be interesting to see what you can do from a running start. You concentrate on your jumping, and if you are good enough I'll take you to a school track and field meet."

Motivated by the coach's encouragement and challenge Bill worked hard at his long jump. True to his promise the coach introduced Bill to a track training session on the following Wednesday and was astounded to see the young man clear sixteen feet and eight inches on his first attempt at the long jump. Bill took third place over all in the Hixson Junior High School elimination trials.

The coach invited Bill, "Would you mind going with the track team to compete at the school's track meet?"

"Sure I will." Bill felt privileged to be considered, and with great enthusiasm accepted the coach's invitation.

Breaking the news of his sporting achievements at home drew a blank. Dad was busy and mom felt Bill was involved in too many sports. She said that he needed to give attention to more academic matters. However, he excelled on the day. In his first experience on the track he competed against the best long jumpers of that school district and jumped seventeen feet and nine inches. Unexpectedly Bill took first place.

This success spurred him on to make sure he was in good shape for the next athletic meet. Each track meet assuaged Bill's craving for more recognition. Like many young men he wanted to do things that made him acceptable to his peers. With every athletic achievement Bill was lettered in all three sports, and he wore his school colors with pride. He knew he was excelling and became even more popular with the school kids. He took particular satisfaction in knowing that at school he was not only recognized as Pastor Bill Stafford's son, he was also known as a promising athlete.

There was only one thing that disappointed Bill. During most of these athletic successes his parents were not present to see how well their son was achieving. Dad was still frequently away from home on his preaching trips while his mother was not able to attend. Little by little his dad's absence increased the animosity Bill felt in his formative mind and heart.

However, Bill did enjoy some of the privileges of being a pastor's son. Even though he was only a teenager, it was largely due to him being a well known pastor's kid that he was voted to be the president of the Fellowship of Christian Athletes. He was also elected to be the vice president of the Student Council at Hixson Junior High School. No one questioned Bill's integrity nor doubted his Christian profession. He was athletic at school and outwardly religious at home. He played football during the week and continued to play a full part in the Sunday activities at the Baptist church. He had the best of both worlds.

Occasionally Bill sustained some strains and pains in his growing physical frame. It was during training for the next track meet that Bill suffered some dull pelvic and lower back pain. The coach told him to rest and not jump until the actual day of the meet. Even though he complied with the coach's advice, the pain persisted, yet Bill insisted in turning out in the school colors.

While he was limbering himself up and preparing for the long jump which had become his specialty, the pain grew more intense and sharp. He tried to ignore the discomfort as he raced toward the lift-off line. As he leaped into the air something suddenly seemed to snap in the upper region of his right leg. A sharp pain shot from his pelvis down into his thigh. Bill fell to the ground like a wet rag and was writhing in pain. A muscle had become detached from his pelvis. The coach plied ice packs around the lower part of his back and hip and then helped carry Bill to the side where they leaned him against a nearby fence.

On that day Dr. Stafford had promised that he would attend that track meet, but there had also been some disagreement about whether Bill should commit himself to yet another sporting event. Besides his academic work suffering at school Mrs. Stafford felt that Bill seemed to be gone all the time, and there were things for him to do at home. Furthermore, she could not afford the time to attend all of Bill's sporting events. Dr. Stafford maintained that children live only once and they should enjoy their sports activities while they are able.

He agreed to attend but as a result of this difference of opinion Dr. Stafford went on his own to support his son at the track meet. However, on the way there he got caught up in a traffic jam. When he finally did arrive he was just in time to find Bill propped up against the fence where the coach had left him and he was still in agony. Immediately Bill took his son to the hospital emergency and accident unit.

Pain-killing drugs were administered to relieve Bill's obvious distress. Dr. Stafford could not help think that if only he and Bill had listened to mom, then Bill would not have gone ahead with the jumping event nor would he be in this mess.

For the next week Bill remained in the hospital and had to lie prostrate on his back with only minimum movement allowed. With the enforced rest his dad was able to spend a lot of quality time with his son that week. This was something they had not done for a long time.

Bill was confined to lie on his back at home for another week before he was allowed to return to school. Even though he returned to school, for the next three months Bill hobbled around on crutches. During this time he underwent thorough physical examinations and physiotherapy to avoid the risk of any serious and permanent damage. This injury brought down the curtains prematurely on Bill's promising track career.

Slipping out of the athletic limelight was a major blow for Bill. The recognition he had gained as an emerging track star had filled a big gap in Bill's life. The welcome applause had fed his ego, and the popular acclaim had filled the vacuum he sensed had been created by his parents' absence and lack of interest in his sporting achievements. With his track involvement finished Bill had to struggle to maintain recognition and acceptance of his peers in other ways.

It was after this summer of injury and trauma that Bill graduated from junior high school to become a sophomore at Hixson High School. Even though he had had to abandon the track and field sports, Bill was still able to play football for Hixson High School. He was a back-up fullback and played on most of the specialty teams such as the kick-off team, return team and the field goal team. During the next year as a junior he was the fullback for the school's starting line up. Bill was a proud member of this team when it made an impressive eight and three for the season and won the Lion Bowl at Tallahoma, Tennessee, during his first year in high school. These successes meant Bill lettered all the way through his three years in high school. He felt he was on top of the world.

Sadly, his arrival at the high school corresponded with Bill's first exposure to drugs. Steve, who was a neighbor to Bill and who also came from a very good home, had been Bill's buddy in ninth grade. Steve's older brother told the two boys how it was cool it was to smoke pot and dabble in other drugs. But the boys knew he had already been caught red handed with drugs and concluded that they would never be so dumb as to be caught with the substances.

However, curiosity got the better of the two pals one day and they decided to experiment with some pot. A third friend bought some of the dehydrated weed and the three of them made their way to a deserted cabin to smoke several joints. After inhaling and puffing through several sticks of pot, they felt no immediate stupefying effect other than an initial horrible sensation of squeamishness. This gave them a false sense of satisfaction and macho pride that encouraged them to smoke some more joints later that evening at a party. For the first time in their young lives the three young men became intoxicated with a drug. This "high" gave them a feeling of exhilaration, and they boasted that they enjoyed the experience.

Bill and Steve also experimented with alcohol, but they did not acquire a taste for it. Bill reasoned with himself and concluded, "They can have their alcohol but I prefer to smoke pot."

Furthermore, Bill felt that getting into drugs would not only be enjoyable but it could earn him some respect as a macho guy at school. This insatiable appetite for recognition amongst his peers drove Bill into many areas that were alien to his upbringing.

However, Bill and Steve took a bigger leap into experimenting with other drugs. A girl introduced Steve to some known junkies from nearby Brainard, and they became a source of a steady supply of an assortment of drugs. At first it was pot and marijuana, but these were soon followed by speed tablets and Quaaludes. All these drugs and narcotics gave the boys a false sense of euphoria and serenity. They were however totally turned off by the idea of injecting dope into their veins.

During a visit to their newly acquired friends in an apartment at Brainard Bill and Steve smoked pot with them until they all got high. Three other guys who sat at a table close by were shooting up with needles into their veins. The two boys from Hixson watched in awe as one young fellow kept slapping his arm and complained that he could not find a vein. He solicited the help of his friends and invited them to inject for him. It was all too much for Steve. Color drained from his face as he broke into a cold sweat. He turned to Bill and said, "I've got to get out of here."

The two boys exited the apartment in a hurry, but as soon as Steve got out to the narrow corridor he collapsed at Bill's feet. Bill was frightened and helped his fainted friend to his feet. With his arm around Steve both struggled out of the apartment block and into the fresh air. The pouring rain was a welcome refresher until Bill was able to help Steve into his car and finally got the air-conditioning going full blast.

This visit to Brainard had definitely turned the two guys against any thought of using needles.

Steve and Bill were soon able to supplement their experiments in illegal drugs by a whole range of regular drugs from medicine cupboards. Within a short time they were sniffing coke, smoking pot and downing brand named tablets. Frequently the powders were produced in homemade laboratories where incompetent amateurs had little control over the potency of the drugs. The youths were not aware of the risks they were running with their health.

Very soon they were not only taking the drugs, they also set up a network for the sale and distribution of drugs at Hixson High School. In this way they were able to minimize the expense of buying their own dope.

Bill and his friends also trafficked in angel dust, downers, "orange goofeys" and acid. All these drugs had the potential of frying a person's brain but the boys were enjoying the kicks. Very soon the two guys were raiding their parents' medicine cupboards and stealing prescription drugs for their personal use.

During Bill's junior year Steve moved away from Hixson to another town. Although he missed Steve Bill soon befriended John who was generally recognized in the school as a Golden Gloves boxer. No one messed around with John. On the contrary, the students generally looked up to him. Bill calculated that his friendship with John would add to his already inflated prestige in the school. John also had an attraction to drugs which contributed to becoming Bill's best friend for years to come. At this stage they were part of a group of boys who continued to flirt with foul language and pornography.

Bill's major problem was that he was living in two worlds and he was trying to win acceptance in both. At school he was running with the wrong crowd and reveled in their unseemly behavior. Back home and during the weekends he courted the religious circle and spoke their language. In front of his parents he did the right things and always tried to please them, and at this time they were unaware of the activities their son got up to away from home.

Every parent likes to think of and expect the best from their children. The guys who came around the Stafford's house with Bill seemed to be fine respectable youths who came from very good homes. Some of them drove gleaming new cars. Mom and dad knew that Bill was impressionable, and very soon he spoke of owning his automobile. He arrived home from school one day and said he did not want to ride on the school bus any more. He wanted a car just like his friends.

Bill's parents had always endeavoured to impart to their five children a sense of individual responsibility. Each one of their children had their household chores: cutting grass, edging the lawns, sweeping leaves, etc. During summer vacations Bill earned a few dollars working at a local grocery store or scooping ice-cream at the Northgate Mall. During one summer he even experienced more strenuous work at a Chattanooga construction company. His parents tried to instill into Bill the value of money in relation to work and ownership. With the money he earned at various jobs and a little help from his dad Bill was able to secure his first car.

Bill and Sue Stafford had no reason to suspect their son would also be spending his money on drugs. At that time they would not have recognized what a drug was. As far as they knew drugs were not part of the church scene, and they were probably a little bit naïve to think that the school system was able to safeguard children from the dangers of drugs. Throughout Bill's adolescent years Dr. Stafford tried to maintain strict Christian disciplines when he was at home. However, although Bill honored these values when at home, they were abandoned at the end of their yard. Worldly encroachments were still off limits in the house. Dr. & Mrs. Stafford insisted that their kids were not allowed to own or play any form of rock or pop music in the home, nor were they allowed to read anything other than wholesome magazines and books. For the other children this did not seem to present a problem but it confined him to more clandestine ways of enjoying his habits.

Dr. and Mrs. Stafford and Bill's sisters Brenda and Karen, formed the Stafford Family Quartet, and besides singing at many churches and conferences they also produced five albums. However, Bill was not into Christian music very much, so he smuggled earphones into his bedroom so that he could listen to the popular songs he knew his friends listened to. Hard rock, acid rock and any form of rock and roll music was popular with Bill and his companions. Vamped up speakers in their cars gave the guys deafening acoustics which they played full blast as they drove around the city streets.

Bill and his friends had several girlfriends during his high school years. Some of these girls indulged in the same wild pursuits as the other guys were getting into. During Bill's senior year in high school he and several of his friends planned to go to a graveyard on Halloween night to play a practical joke on their girlfriends. Before going to the cemetery the guys had been smoking pot so most of them were pretty high. In the cemetery all the guys lay on top of the graves. Later a friend led the unsuspecting girls on a short cut through the graveyard. In the darkness the motionless bodies of the guys suddenly came alive and the guys acted as if they were going to grab the girls as they ran by. The frightened girls ran off screaming into the night.

They made so much noise that someone who lived nearby called the police. As the guys and girls left the graveyard they formed a line of six cars at the front of which was Bill's. Just down the road and over the top of the first hill they met about five police cars on the way to the cemetery. Three patrol cars whizzed by in the direction of the graveyard but two other cars pulled over in front of Bill who was leading the way.

Bill had an ounce of pot in the car. As soon as they saw the police Bill's friend threw the pot out the car window and it landed about four or five cars back. The police made all the gang get out of their vehicles. The officers checked out all the guys and their cars but found nothing. They then began searching beside and underneath the cars. They went up and down the road looking for anything that the young people might have thrown out. Bill's heart was beating fast fearing what the officers might find.

After what seemed to be forever the police finally let them all go but told them to go straight home. Instead of obeying the police order all the kids went to a restaurant and excitedly talked about the whole ordeal.

The next day Bill and his friend went back to see if they could find the small bag of pot. They discovered the bag still intact and lying just where the last car had been parked. The two boys could not believe that the police officers had not found it.

These escapes from the arm of the law did not deter Bill from continuing with his habit. One weekend the Staffords had a family get-together at the parents' home. Unknown to his mom and dad, Bill had a quarter pound of pot under the seat of his car which was parked at the side of the house. After some time a family member indicated that they had to leave early. Bill was unaware that his car was blocking the vehicle that was to leave. His sister Brenda, who lived in the nearby trailer home on the farm, volunteered to move Bill's car.

When Brenda slid into the driver's seat and put the car into gear, the bag of pot jolted out from under the bench seat. Until this point, although mom and dad had an idea that young Bill was doing drugs, this was the first time they had tangible evidence. Bill was severely chastised for this discovery, but like many other reprimands it failed to alter his ways.

After a football game during Bill's senior year he and his friends returned to an apartment for an all night party. At this all-night spree Bill had his first experience with a hallucinating drug named "windowpane," which in the drug culture, is known as "Acid." There is no way to describe the feeling. At first Bill thought his heart was going to burst, and then came the hallucination. The things he saw or thought he saw were weird. Ornaments and pictures on the wall seemed to melt before his eyes. This drug was so strong that it made sleep virtually impossible that night. Bill was only one of two guys who took the "windowpane" that night. Someone took the other guy home, and everyone else fell asleep around three and four o'clock in the morning.

While everyone else was sleeping Bill lay on a sofa and watched television until the programs finished. With glazed eyes he stared at the snow-like distortion on the screen until he heard his friend's mother come in around five o'clock. Bill faked as though he was asleep. The lady turned the television off. Bill lay there with no one to talk to and nothing to watch until the day finally dawned. When the effects of the drug wore off Bill felt as though his brain had been fried.

On another night Bill did finally think that his number was up and he was going to die. He and three other guys met a pusher and bought a dime of "Match Head T" which was a morphine based powder. They split the powder into "nickels" and each used a dollar to snort the morphine powder. Prior to going into the auditorium for a school basketball game they drove around school perimeter several times before finally abandoning the car in the parking lot. Bill staggered from the automobile, and with his friends he scrambled up onto the bleachers to cheer the school team. During the course of the game Bill felt he was drifting into oblivion. Everything seemed to darken, and he knew something was seriously wrong. He became completely dysfunctional even though his eyes remained wide open.

Bill has no recollection of how he got down from the bleachers but his friends must have carried him out to John's car where they laid him out on the back seat. In his dazed state he thought he was in danger of not making it. He spoke to John and George, John's cousin, "If I don't make it, please tell mom and dad that I love them."

George had not taken any drugs but he was frightened to see his two friends in such a desperate state. He decided to drive them up Highway 27 to Bakewell with windows of the car fully open in the hope of the fresh air reviving Bill and John. During the drive George tried to carry on a conversation with his drugged passengers, for he was afraid and anxious lest either of the two boys should die. They were blocked out.

Little by little the young men began to recover, and eventually George was able to drive Bill to his parents' home. George and John were relieved to discover that Dr. & Mrs. Stafford were not at home. The two friends helped Bill to his bedroom and left hastily. When Bill awoke next morning he was still seeing black spots and flashes of light in his eyes.

The incident frightened Bill, but he was hooked and could not break his fatal attraction for drugs even though he knew they were doing him harm. He was experiencing the truth expressed in the maxim, "The chains of habit are too weak to be felt until they are too strong to be broken."

Smoking joints before a football game was the cool thing to do so Bill joined with the other players and inhaled the stupefying weed. Again, after a football game, the players would take off with the guys to party at a nearby Pizza Hut. Frequently the party continued to the wee hours of the morning. One such incident occurred when Hixson was playing Soddy Daisy High School, and the score was tied 0-0 in the second quarter. Bill got the call to go straight up the middle. He took the handoff and ran straight up the middle of the field. He was hit once by a linebacker of the opposing team. Bill spun off the burly player, ran into another player and spun off him also. When he looked up he saw no one around so took off running up the sideline toward the goal. When he was on the four yard line someone grabbed him around the collar. This was the last defender that had any chance of stopping Bill scoring. The opponent dived at Bill and slung him out of bounds. As he fell over out of bounds the opponent pulled Bill backwards and Bill's feet got caught underneath his own body. As a result of the fall Bill pulled a thigh muscle, and he was out the rest of the game. The Hixson High schoolers scored two plays later and won the ballgame. Bill had a lot of satisfaction that he had contributed to that goal, but after the game he was in severe pain.

Bill arrived at the Pizza Hut after the game where he met up with the same guys who generally partied with him. They gave Bill some Quaaludes to help with the pain. Under the influence of these drugs Bill became oblivious to any pain and continued to party into the early hours of the following morning.

Seldom was any one awake at the Stafford home when Bill arrived after these parties nor was he asked the next morning why he got home so late. In conversation the next day he would tell his family or Margaret about the ball game the previous evening but never mentioned the horrendous parties.

Several times when Bill's mom and dad were away from home conducting revivals in some distant city the young ball players would arrived at the Stafford's Northwoods home with their sports gear. They were Bill's guests, and they lived it up all night while his mom and dad were absent and totally ignorant of these wild sprees.

When Bill was a senior at Hixson High School he was in the starting line up of the school team to play the final game of the year. It was to be the last of his football career. Although Bill was already heavily involved in drugs, he was also surprised to discover how freely drugs seemed to be used amongst those engaged in the various school sports programs.

Just before Bill went to the field house to dress for this final game, he and one of his friends found a dead-end street where they smoked about six joints of pot. When they walked into that field house they were high and their closest teammates knew it. After the game Bill and his friends went to the Pizza Hut on Hixson Pike. This was their regular hang out. From there Bill met up with other drug-taking friends and went to an apartment where they got high. Under the influence of these drugs the kids partied almost all night during which they experimented with all sorts of other dope.

By the time Bill was ready to graduate from Hixson High School, he was not only a drug pusher, he was also hooked on dope. For three years he had been dabbling in drugs and already they were taking a heavy toll on his young life. He had enjoyed the thrill of acceptance amongst the toughest group at the high school but he had no academic achievements to show for his years at school.

It came as a shock to his parents to learn that their son, who was popular with his peers, was not going to graduate with the class of '75 from Hixson High School. The school reports they had received indicated that Bill was on course for graduation. They discovered too late that Bill had altered the reports before taking them home. It hit them like a ton of bricks when Bill came home and said he had failed his English course and was not able to join his friends at the school graduation in May 1975.

He attended summer school that same year and was able to pass his G. E. D. exams and gain a school diploma. However, while others were applying for entrance to college and university, Bill got a job scooping ice-cream at Baskin Robins. He had no interest in academics. During that last year at school his parents had purchased an eighty acre farm in Bradley county and had gone there to live. Bill had no interest in working at the farm either. He wanted to enjoy the good life which he mistakenly thought was found in drugs and worldly revelry.

CHAPTER 4
TAKING THE HIGH ROAD

Dr. Bill Stafford was being greatly used of God at Bible conferences all across America, and even more churches in many states were requesting his ministry. However, Dr. Bill and his wife Sue longed to see their children following in the ways of the Savior. They were aware that young Bill was leading a double life. Dad tried to reason with his son how important it was to be one hundred per cent for the Lord. The painful thing was that Bill agreed with his Dad. He answered nearly every altar call at his church but all the while he still was running with the wrong bunch.

Ron, a former school friend at Hixson, was studying at East Tennessee State University in Johnson City, Tennessee. Periodically Bill and his friends rode up to Johnson City to visit their old friend. With little or no restraints on their behavior and in a different environment, the guys had an absolute ball. On one occasion they arranged for Ron to buy tickets for them all to attend a concert at the Freedom Hall in Johnson City where the infamous Black Sabbath group was performing.

The guys bought a few packets of brownie mix and baked it with marijuana. They smuggled the adulterated brownies and some pot into the Freedom Hall. Bill and his buddies were overwhelmed with the occasion. They were enthralled with Ozzy Osbourne and his sidekicks on their electric guitars, drums and electric piano blasting out blasphemous and satanic lines over a mammoth audio system. Thousands of teenagers around them swayed and swooned in the balmy air. It was evident that many of those present were junkies or kids living on the edge of drug abuse. The whole atmosphere was totally foreign to anything Bill had ever known back at the Baptist church in Chattanooga.

Sadly, Bill Stafford had chosen to be part of this drug generation. The visits to Johnson City spurred Bill and his chums on to revel in the music of other rock musicians and heavy metal singers such as Leonard Skynard, Ted Nugent and Led Zepplin.

Drugs and rock music are well suited to each other. The heavy beat of guitars and percussion instruments seemed to almost hypnotize the guys when they smoked pot. Most of Bill's money was spent either on drugs or buying cassettes of his favorite singers.

"Come on over to our house. There's no one at home and my mom and dad won't be back for several days." said Bill to his friends.

The preacher's house became the venue for wild parties which lasted into the small hours of the morning. The familiar surroundings where his dad's voice was heard in prayer for his children was desecrated by foul language, the swigging of cans of beer, smoking pot and snorting dope. Sadly, young Bill Stafford had no second thoughts about it. He was enjoying the good life with the drug crowd. He always thought that his parents were too prudish and old fashioned in their values.

The next day Bill would tidy the house, leaving open all doors to eliminate any lingering odors from the previous evening's party. His unsuspecting parents would arrive home totally unaware of what had transpired at their house during their absence.

However, news of the frequent house parties soon got back to Dr. Stafford. Teenage parties were one thing, but drugs in their house would not be tolerated. If drugs were found in their home, it would send the wrong message to the rest of the family. Bill's behavior seemed to be paradoxical to his parents. On one hand he appeared to be a clean living young man who loved sports, respected his parents and attended church every week. However, his involvement in drugs and the associated behavior did not seem to be consistent. Dr. Stafford and his wife took much more time focusing on Bill in light of his obvious waywardness.

In spite of their repeated warnings Bill chose to ignore his parents advice and persisted in his willful indulgence. They had tried to train and shape Bill's life, but they could not control his behavior. He had made certain choices in his life which were contrary to the values held in the Stafford home. It was tough love that made Bill and Sue Stafford take more drastic measures to help their son though the firmness was painful. It was then that Bill's mom and dad decided that Bill should be given the ultimatum to either straighten up or to move out. This was not rejection; it was administration of bitter medicine which the parents hoped would help sort out Bill's problems. It was also the best choice for the family.

Bill did not see any need for a dose of parental medicine. He had chosen to leave home and to move in with his best friend's family in Hixson. John and Bill had shared mutual interests in the school's sports program. John had also gained the added distinction of being a Golden Gloves' boxer. In spite of their involvement in sports, both of them were entangled in the drug web, and both seemed to be well on the way to becoming addicts. Furthermore, Bill was now unrestricted by any parental authority and did not have to conform and act like a preacher's kid.

On the day that Bill faced his father's ultimatum and made his decision to leave home, he met up with John in the Mount Vernon Baptist Church parking lot. As was prearranged they arrived at John's house with Bill's car fully laden. It was not unusual for Bill to stay over at John's home. They had been best pals at school. After they unpacked the car the two boys sat on the floor in John's room and Bill poured out his account of what had led to his eviction from home. He confessed to John that he could not live any longer under his parents' jurisdiction. The regime was too restrictive. When his dad had given the ultimatum to shape up or ship out, he had had no alternative but to leave.

John's dad sat with the two boys in their living room and again Bill and John painted a dismal picture of Bill's hardships at home which had John's parents looking pitifully on the preacher's kid. They offered him a bed as long as he needed to stay.

Back home in Bradley County Bill and Sue Stafford had heavy hearts. They did not sleep that night nor for weeks to come, and during this time Bill did not leave their thoughts and prayers. Dr. Stafford continued to travel to revivals which had been arranged months before. One night while he stayed in a motel the burden was so great that he paced the floor and cried to God.

Dr. Stafford relates,

> I felt such a great oppression of heart that I could not sleep. Sometimes I was down on my knees at the side of the bed. When not kneeling, I walked up and down the room talking and crying to the Lord. I only got peace in my heart when God gave me two promises from His Word; "Believe on the Lord Jesus Christ, and thou shalt be saved, and thy house." (Acts 16:31); "The Lord is not slack concerning his promise, as some men count slackness; but is longsuffering to us-ward, not willing that any should perish, but that all should come to repentance." (II Peter 3:9) These two verses came to me with great impact. It was as if God was giving me something to hold on to. After that I had to learn to appropriate these promises in spite of Bill's waywardness.

Having somewhere to stay solved one problem, but Bill still needed money to survive. John's Dad offered to help and spoke to a friend who arranged a job for Bill at Abilities Incorporated where he learned how to make pallets. He started at $2.25 per hour. It was not great money, but Bill felt this would help until he found something better.

After several months at John's house, Brian, another young man who had become a close friend, invited Bill to move into a small rented house in Cowart Street, Chattanooga. Another young man who shared in the same house was Keith. Keith and Bill soon became best friends.

Bill's problems with drugs were not getting any better. Bill, John and Keith not only purchased drugs for their own use, but they also sold drugs to various clients. They learned to make the strong cocaine go farther by mixing it with baby laxative and increasing the mass. They were able to sell this and make sufficient profit to finance the demands of their own habit. The money they earned pushing drugs also financed the wild parties where the guys and girls got high and partied the night away. These crazy parties were held either in the small house at Cowart Street or at various night clubs in Chattanooga. Inevitably these reckless parties led to unrestrained promiscuity.

One Friday night Bill met up with a friend who was playing in a rock band at Charlie Brown's, a Chattanooga night club. At the interval the two guys and a young woman decided to step outside the club and smoke a few joints of pot. As Bill walked to his car he noticed two police cars across the street in the restaurant's parking lot.

Bill got into his car and pulled out on to Brainard Road. He noticed in his mirror that the two police cars had pulled out behind him. Bill told his friends not to light up because they were being followed. After travelling half a mile down the road Bill pulled the car into a parking lot at the "IHOP" (International House of Pancakes.) Bill was alarmed when the cops followed them into the same parking lot with their blue lights flashing.

Two police officers, a lady and a man, hurried out of their car just as Bill also emerged from his vehicle. He recognized the cops because they had been after him before. It seemed to Bill that the male officer had a personal vendetta against him because he had dated the cop's girlfriend some months earlier. Bill was sure this officer wanted to bust him pretty badly. The cops ignored the two passengers but forced Bill to undergo several tests to measure any level of intoxication. Both officers shouted their commands in quick succession at Bill like bullets firing from a gun. "Touch your nose. Stand on one foot. Put your head back. Look straight ahead."

Somehow Bill was able to pass all their tests even though he knew he was high from dope he had taken earlier. The officers looked quizzically at each other and the female cop asked her buddy what he wanted to do. The officer replied, "I guess we have to let him go."

Bill and his friends were released. If the police had searched the car they would have found plenty of evidence to arrest Bill and his two friends. They had several ounces of pot ready for smoking plus fifty hits of Quaaludes in the car's air conditioning vent.

After several low paying jobs Bill finally found steady employment at the Siskin Steel & Supply Company in the city. The hours suited him perfectly, for it meant he could continue to party most nights and still work at his day-time job. However, drug addicts are compelled to feed their voracious craving and burning lust for more drugs. After the late night parties Bill needed to take regular hits of speed during the following day to be able to stay awake and work at his job. During the lunch break some workers had a pizza or a burger, but Bill usually spent the hour treating himself to drinking "wild turkey" and smoking pot.

Bill's weekends were much like his weeks but worse. His weekend was just one long continuous binge. On the way home from work at four o'clock on Friday afternoon Bill stopped by the liquor store to pick up some alcoholic drinks to help him and his friends enter into the swing and mood for the weekend party. After a shower and change of clothes Bill and his two companions treated themselves to a Jack Daniel's (a glass of whiskey and coke) and they smoked some pot. In the slang they called it "catching a buzz" which meant they were priming themselves up for the weekend spree.

The guys then headed to O'Grady's Night Club to meet up with other guys and girls who were also caught up with alcohol and drugs. The dim lights and disco dancing enhanced the feel-good factor. Even though they were drugged and intoxicated Bill seldom lost control of his faculties. He could drink large quantities of alcohol and consume considerable doses of drugs and not appear to be intoxicated.

After ten o'clock in the evening Bill and his buddies would leave O'Grady's and head to several other night clubs in Chattanooga. The Tiki Hut, the Sport's Page the Night Deposit and Charlie Brown's, are only a few of the locations frequented by these party-goers. On most nights they picked girls up at the clubs and after the clubs and bars closed at two o'clock in the morning the party-goers returned to their houses to continue their high jinks throughout the night.

Most of them fell asleep only after the sun dawned on Saturday morning. They slept in beds, on couches or on the floor until early on Saturday afternoon. By late afternoon they were then ready to repeat the cycle of drink, drugs and clubs right through Saturday night and well into Sunday morning. Sometimes they continued the spree all day Sunday without any sleep and finally collapsed in exhaustion early on Monday morning.

During all this time Bill visited his family twice each month on Sunday afternoons. Dr. Bill Stafford recalls those visits,

> When Bill came home he looked like a corpse. He was unkempt, skinny, unshaven and his blond hair was long. We were sure he had not slept for days. He certainly looked dazed. Bill refused to accompany us to church, preferring to spend Sunday by the swimming pool. He had abandoned all contact with any church. We did not nag about what he was doing or what he should not do, but our hearts were breaking and yearning for our son to return to the Lord. Not only were we praying we also solicited the prayers of close friends.
>
> Before Bill left I usually would go to his car and assure him that we loved him and were praying for him. Sometimes I quoted to him the promises God had given to us. At other times I told him that sin was a hard taskmaster and would always catch up with him. He always listened respectfully.

Bill recalls those trips home,

> Mom and Dad had something that I could never
> attain. They were busy people, but they were com-
> passionate. They had high standards, but they did not
> impose them on me when I went to hang around the
> home on Sundays. I was often touched and embar-
> rassed by my Dad's brokenness when he would hug
> me at the car and say, "Son, if you died and went to
> hell I can't see how heaven can be really perfect with-
> out you. Mama and I love you and pray for you con-
> tinually." Tears were in daddy's eyes and sometimes
> in my eyes too when he spoke like that to me.

Mom and dad's prayers were undoubtedly what saved Bill
from many threatening and perilous situations. However, Bill did
not give credit to such praying. He thought he got through by his
own cleverness and with the help of friends. One girl whom Bill
dated for quite a while was a secretary at the District Attorney's
Office. She was able to glean information about who was under
surveillance or who was about to be indicted. She was able to tip
Bill off, and he relayed the information to his friends.

These guys lived on their wits from week to week.
However, there was one day when no one tipped Bill off that he
was being watched. He stopped by the drug dealer as he did most
Friday afternoons and bought a quarter pound of pot, fifty hits of
Quaaludes and one hundred hits of speed. This was a small quota
for the weekend spree. Generally it was double this amount.

As Bill neared the house he shared with Brian and Keith he
noticed an unmarked car coming in the opposite direction. Bill
slowly made a right into their street and noticed that the
unmarked car turned left into the same street and was following
behind Bill. Half way down the street Bill swung his car into the
driveway of their house. As he turned he noticed that the other
car quickly accelerated into the neighbor's driveway which ran

parallel to Bill. The unmarked car pulled over to cut Bill off before he could reach the house.

Puzzled by what was happening Bill opened his car door and was startled to see two guys briskly emerging out of the unmarked vehicle and coming towards him. "Get out!" they screamed at Bill who froze on the spot. The officers brandished their police badges and announced that they were plain clothes officers from the City Narcotic Department. They took Bill's keys and locked the doors of his car. Bill was spread-eagled up against his car while an officer searched his clothing. Bill's heart was racing and his mind jumped to several conclusions. He was sure he had been finally busted. When they start to search the car I will be taken straight to jail.

"What is that in your pocket?" barked one of the officers.

The other officer removed a few dollars change that Bill had stuffed into his pocket after buying the dope. After searching his person and finding no narcotic substance they secured Bill and marched him to the front door of the house. One officer banged the door. Bill knew that Keith and Brian would be at home.

One of the boys shouted from inside, "Who is it?"

"Cops." replied an officer. Keith opened the door immediately. He was not able to conceal his apprehension and bewilderment. One officer ordered Bill and Keith to sit down. While he stood guard over the two guys the other officer began to search the house.

When the cop who searched the house discovered Brian was in the shower he hollered for him to get out of the bathroom immediately. The officer kept banging on the door. Brian delayed in opening the door while he grabbed some clothes. Meanwhile the impatient officer took out a knife and tried to prize the door open. He was afraid lest Brian was trying to flush any drugs down the toilet.

While the officer was still trying to force the door open Brian unlocked the bolt. He was standing in his underwear. "Hey, what is this?" Brian questioned.

"Where are the drugs?" the officer demanded. It so happened Brian was as clean as a whistle. He was not into drugs like Bill and Keith.

Brian replied, "What drugs? I don't have any drugs."

Even though he was still in his underpants Brian was taken into the living room to join Bill and Keith who remained under the custody of the other cop. The officer began to tear the house apart hunting for narcotics. Drawers and cupboards were emptied. Wall panels were loosened and it seemed that no stone was left unturned. He searched in every nook and cranny, but no drugs were to be found in the house. The officer guarding the three guys left them momentarily to join the other policeman in the kitchen where they could be heard discussing their next move.

While their guard was absent Bill winked over at Keith to get his attention. He then mouthed inaudibly to his friend, "In my car. They are in my car."

Keith had already been busted for drugs when he and a school friend went to Florida on a school senior's trip several years earlier. They had tried to purchase a pound of pot only to discover they had walked into a trap set up by a police narcotic unit. The two boys were charged with possession of drugs and taken to court where for their first offense and as a result were put on several years' probation. Keith was afraid that if these officers should discover drugs in Bill's car he might go to jail. Bill also was quaking of what might happen if they searched his automobile.

Just then one of the officers received an urgent call on his radio. He asked the guys if he could use their phone. Consent was readily given. The police officer spoke excitedly down the phone within earshot of the three guys. Evidently another narcotic case demanded urgent attention, and the officer assured the person on the other end of the line that they would be there immediately.

As the officers walked out through the porch one of them tossed the car keys back to Bill and said, "Keep it clean guys. We'll be back."

With that they jumped into their car and sped off down the road.

All the boys gave expressions of great relief. Bill's heart was still pounding but he was dumbfounded. "How did we escape?" he thought.

Brian assured Bill and Keith that they had been lucky but in the back of Bill's mind was the thought that God had spared his praying parents from the grief and embarrassment of their boy being up in court on a drug charge.

This incident left Bill paranoid about being caught by the cops, but it was not sufficient to discourage him from continuing to take and push drugs. The drug habit began like wrapping thin threads of pleasure around his life. Now the threads had been woven into a strong addiction that he could not break. Within a few days he was as unworried and irresponsible as before about his involvement in narcotics.

It was within a short time following this incident that Brian, the owner of the house the guys lived in, proposed marriage to one of the girls he had met at one of their wild parties. In view of the bride soon coming to the house Keith and Bill moved out to Mountain Creek Apartments, Redbank, on the outskirts of Chattanooga.

From their new residence the two guys continued to traffic drugs to various customers. Some nights they went from one night club to another selling drugs to the proprietors, barmaids, entertainers and any one who would buy them. Several popular Tennessee entertainers considered Bill and Keith to be their close buddies.

Backstage in the dressing rooms, before the show and during the interval, these guys joined Bill and Keith to snort cocaine and smoke joints so that they got real high. They then returned to play their music. On most nights after the show the rock groups went back to Bill and Keith's apartment for more drugs and alcohol. The camaraderie with these popular rock bands assuaged Bill's continued desire for recognition and acceptance.

Along the way there were some stark reminders how perilous was the path Bill had chosen. One evening he and friends were playing poker and getting euphoric on dope when someone knocked on the door. Having checked through the spy eye in the door who the caller was they admitted him to their den. The friend told them some sad news about Tom, one of their young teenage friends. Tom and his three older brothers frequently joined Bill and others to experiment with various drugs. However, the three brothers were constantly feuding with several brothers from another family.

That night the caller told Bill and Keith that Tom and a friend had gone to the Bowling Alley on Hixson Pike. In a parking lot they spied a motor bike which belonged to a brother from the rival family. Tom and his companion stole the motor bike and sped across the parking lot towards the Hixson Pike. It is not known if young Tom was high on drugs or not. He never stopped at a busy intersection leading on to the main highway and drove head-on into a car. He was killed instantly. Bill and his friends were stunned. They could not believe it. It was a salutary warning to Bill of the nearness of eternity even for young people. Sadly, such reminders of eternity were quickly quenched by the lure of Bill's company and what he considered to be the good life.

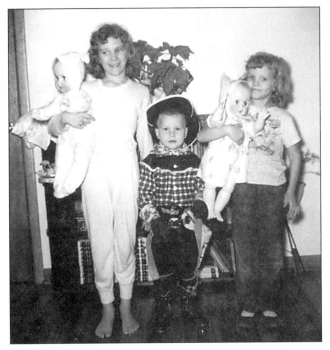

Brenda, Bill, & Karen (Bill III - 4yrs.)

Bill playing game with older brother Bobby.

Dad, Mom, Brenda, & Karen
(Bill III - 2yrs.)

Bill Stafford III

Stafford Family (Bill III - 12 yrs.)

Bill III, Senior Year (17 yrs.)

Bill III, Senior Year,
Starting Fullback

Bill III getting handoff from childhood friend, Jeff Chaffin.

*Bill III at Glen Haven Baptist giving testimony
just a few months after conversion.*

Christmas at the farm

Bill III

Older sister Karen's Wedding, Steve Stafford on far left.
Next to him is Steve Morris—Bill's best friend.

From left: Lawrence Hailey (Judy's father), Bill & Judy,
Bill & Sue Stafford. Dec. 19, 1987 Jena, LA

Bill & Judy Stafford

*Bill and Judy's daughters Starla
Suzanne and Trisha Lynn*

Standing from left: Dr. Paige Patterson, Ron Lowery, Bill Stafford III,
Seated: Dr. W.A. Criswell

Lupton Drive
Baptist Church

Bill III with two pastors from South Africa
at ICR Conference.

1st ICR Conference in Ireland. These are the participants of the conference—both pastors from Ireland and Americans.

Left: Bill III and Bill Jr. working together at conference.

Bill III speaking at Ireland conference.

CHAPTER 5
HITTING ROCK BOTTOM

The phone rang in the Stafford's farmhouse. Mrs. Stafford answered the call. The man on the other end of the phone asked to speak to Dr. Stafford. Sue Stafford explained that her husband had gone to Alabama for special revival meetings. To this the caller said, "How can your husband be out doing revival meetings when your son was seen coming out of a night club absolutely dazed and under the influence of drugs? Your husband should not be in the ministry."

The voice was sharp. The words were searing. Mrs. Stafford was taken back and could say little other than to reply that her husband was not at home. Sue Stafford put the phone down and dissolved into tears. She was deeply hurt and demoralized. She did not know what motivated the caller. People easily fall into the trap of criticizing a family in crisis rather than supporting and praying for that family. Carrying the burden of a wayward son had already taken a heavy toll on Mrs. Stafford. Now the censure of Christians on her husband's ministry seemed almost unbearable.

Sue punched in the phone number of her husband's motel. Bill had just returned from the evening revival meeting where God had been blessing. His wife just unloaded to him all her pent up feelings down the phone. When she relayed to her husband the brutal allegation made by the unkind person who called their home Bill was stunned. Like Sue, he too was both hurt and felt betrayed and defeated in his life. For some time his soul had been in anguish for his prodigal son. Bill was a jovial person to all who met him, but on the inside his heart was breaking for what was happening in his family.

He and Sue talked for a long time on the phone. "Sue, I think I'll pack it all in," said Bill. "We can't go on like this. It is ruining our lives. On one hand we are trying to serve the Lord, and on the other we are seeing Bill go to the Devil. Now people want to put us in legalistic shackles. Maybe I'll just come home and work on the farm."

"But honey, Bill is not a child. He has left home, and we have no control over his life. What about the promises God has given us?" Sue reasoned.

"We'll talk it over when I get home. Keep on praying honey," said Bill trying to encourage his wife.

Keep on praying? Bill thought it over. Lord we have been praying for nine years and nothing seems to be happening. There was almost a sentiment of complaint in Bill's thoughts toward the Lord.

There was no way Dr. Stafford could go to sleep that night. He knelt at the side of the bed and poured out his heart before God in prayer. The preacher was in distress of soul. He pleaded, he wept, he complained, he yearned, but the burden did not seem to diminish. Still on his knees the preacher asked God to examine his heart. Again he surrendered his ministry to the Lord and indicated that he was prepared to walk away from it all if God so desired.

He tried to appropriate the promises God had given him from the Scriptures on the day that Bill left home, "Believe on the Lord Jesus Christ, and thou shalt be saved, and thy house." (Acts 16:31) and "The Lord is not slack concerning his promise, as some men count slackness; but is longsuffering to us-ward, not willing that any should perish, but that all should come to repentance." (II Peter 3:9)

The night hours slipped by slowly. Daylight began to stream through the window, and the preacher was still in prayer. Dr. Stafford remembers,

> Just as the dawn began to break, it seemed the burden began to lift. Suddenly a surge of peace filled my heart and a new confidence gave to me an assurance that God would answer prayer. I could hardly

wait to phone Sue and tell her all was going to be well. Furthermore, I felt that God had given me a green light to continue in the ministry He had committed to me. He had not chosen me because I was perfect. He knew I wasn't even before I started to preach. I learned again that my ministry did not depend on my perfection but on the sufficiency of Jesus Christ.

Fathers are not necessarily failures because their children rebel. If that were true, then God who is the Father of us all would be considered a failure. Like the father in the parable of the Prodigal Son in the New Testament, parents should keep loving their lost sons and daughters; moms and dads can only pray and wait patiently.

Following this prayer crisis the situation did not improve for young Bill Stafford. Things got even worse. What had started out as doing something for kicks when several guys, barely into their teens, experimented with a few drugs, had now grown to become a fearful monster that threatened to take Bill Stafford and his friends to a premature grave. It was not that Bill did not know what drugs were doing to his body. He just didn't care. Bill was trapped. He knew no other way of living and yet drugs had robbed him of his youth, emptied his pockets, drained his body and almost cast him on the scrap heap of humanity.

There was an overabundance of drugs available. Some were laboratory prepared medicines which carried brand names. These were either stolen or obtained by forged prescriptions. Many others were home manufactured powders prepared in makeshift labs by nonprofessionals at the rear of a garage or work shop. These homemade drugs were often bungled in the preparation process. This would result in them being either low or almost lethal in potency.

Bill became the victim of some over loaded drugs and on several occasions sailed very close to death. One evening after supper he took a counterfeit Quaalude and went to join his friends at the Tiki Hut. After a short while he felt excessively sleepy. He tried to shake himself out of it and staggered across the floor. He realized there was something wrong. He was losing control of his faculties. He left the night club and clambered into his car. He tried to drive down the road towards home, but he was becoming totally dysfunctional. Somehow he made it home to Redbank without crashing the vehicle.

When he woke up next morning he got a call from the girl he was dating. She was concerned to know how he was and announced that she was coming over to the apartment. When she arrived the girlfriend asked Bill how his car came to be parked some distance down the street. Bill had no recollection why he should have abandoned the automobile at this place. On examination he discovered the car was out of gas and he must have had to ditch it where it was. But he had no recollection of how he got from the car to the apartment.

At twenty-four years old drugs had reduced Bill's life to a nonsense. His weight was down. He was emaciated and derelict in his appearance. He became angry with people telling him he looked like death warmed over. For nine years he had been on drugs, and life seemed to be a big merry-go-round that would not stop nor slow down sufficiently for Bill to get off. He had lost out on a career in sports which at one time seemed promising. Dope had denied him his college education and any ambition of a professional life. He was doing drugs seven days a week and partying virtually every night.

His life style became a pernicious cycle of taking stronger drugs to alleviate the despair he felt because he was a drug addict. Bill began to hallucinate. One evening at Bud's Beer Joint he snorted extra strong Angel Dust. He lost control of himself. He was not able to walk. He saw the curtains dissolve before his eyes and turn into all sorts of colors. In the hallucinations he began to see weird things that he had always heard he might see.

People became like animals before him. He thought his mind was going to explode.

His girlfriend brought him out of Bud's Beer Joint and propped him up against a wall in the cooler air of the night. Bill insisted that the girlfriend take him to the car. She was as crazy as he was, for she joined him in the passenger seat of the automobile. Bill tried to reverse the car several times without success. Finally the security guard at Bud's Beer Joint who Bill knew as a fellow drug taker, leaned in through the window of the car and asked Bill, "Are you going to be all right? This is what drugs do to you."

The guard talked Bill into allowing the girlfriend to drive him home. Before reaching the house Bill was totally unconscious and did not surfaced until sometime the next day to repeat the cycle of taking more drugs to face another day.

When Bill had started drugs nine years earlier, he was motivated to gain self esteem amongst his peers. Now as an addict he was hooked on the narcotics because of boredom and seeking something to help him cope with life. He knew no other life. The only friends he had were fellow addicts. Bill was now scraping the bottom of the barrel. His life was empty, and he was craving for something better without knowing what it was.

Bill shared his despair with John and Keith, and although they could understand how he felt, they had no answers to his problems. Religion was never mentioned between Bill and his friends. Keith came from a Christian home, but like Bill, he had abandoned church and all religious trappings. John had no religious affiliation at all.

The boys had many girlfriends whom they met mostly on the weekends. Most of them were casual relationships which they never took too seriously nor for too long. Like the guys, the girls also were out for a good time on the town and some of them were also drug addicts.

When one of these girls invited Bill to go to church with her, he was totally amazed. At first his mind drew a blank, for he had not been in a church for five years. When he did go with the girl he was even more confused. When Bill had attended church he had become accustomed to independent Baptist form of worship. At this meeting people stood with their arms raised in the air and sometimes swaying as they sang the swinging songs. Only later did he learn that this was a charismatic church—a new phenomenon for Bill.

As with many previous sweethearts, the relationship with this girlfriend soon ended, but the impact of being back at church remained with him. He concealed his thoughts about God, religion and eternity from the guys who were closest to him. For Bill to express any thought of religion to his companions in drugs would have stigmatized him as "a bummer," and he was not prepared for that sort of reputation.

In all the years he had been doing drugs no one other than his parents had ever spoken to him about Jesus Christ. He remembered how he had been embarrassed by a Christian six years previously when with his brother Steven he accompanied his mom and dad to Grand Junction, Colorado. Dad had been conducting revival meetings at a tent while the family stayed at a large ranch. It was just about the time that the Staffords had moved to the Bradley County farm and they had special interest in horses.

Bill had sneaked off to a quiet part of the ranch near a river and had smoked some dope he had secretly brought with him. He had gotten high but had remained outdoors to help the drug odor dissipate. His mom and dad were not wise to the smell of drugs at that time and remained unsuspecting.

That evening at the revival meeting a man who was a rustic street evangelist, must have been suspicious of Bill. He looked at the preacher's kid with eagle eyes and challenged him, "Have you ever been saved?"

"Yes." Bill lied to the stranger knowing full well he had long since lost interest in church.

The Colorado revival was the last occasion at which Bill had heard his dad preach. Now six years later, he longed for a change in his life, but he could see no way to free himself from the addiction that gripped him or from the friends that surrounded him. He tried to "grab for all the gusto" as a popular beer commercial encouraged, but there was no gusto there to grab. For nine years he had lived for drugs, women and worldly pursuits, but now they had lost their attraction and fascination for the young man. He had gone from one night club to another in a vain attempt to fill the emptiness of his heart, but his life was even more empty than when he began.

Even though he maintained his daily routine of drugs, clubs and entertainment, he was at a crisis in his life without knowing what was about to happen. In a strange way God was answering his mom and dad's prayers.

Chapter 6
Picking Up
the Broken Pieces

It is always better to batten down the hatches before the storm breaks rather than pick up the pieces after a shipwreck. Bill and Sue Stafford had tried to train up their children in godly ways and teach them eternal values. They were not perfect, and like all parents, they knew more about rearing children and handling teenagers after the family had grown and left home.

Although their son Bill had made shipwreck of his life, they never gave up praying for him. During the nine years in which Bill was sowing his wild oats in the drug scene, buckets of tears soaked Sue Stafford's pillow at night as she pondered and prayed for her boy.

Not only were their hearts constantly opened to heaven in prayer for Bill, they always left the door at home open for him to return at any time. Even though his appearance reflected the drug culture in which he continued, they welcomed him home for Sunday lunch when he came.

In the summer of 1980, after partying the Saturday night away until daylight dawned next morning, Bill made his way to the home farm. He pulled up a chair and slept at the side of the pool. The following day there was small conversation over lunch, but obviously Bill was far away in his mind. He was still reeling from the heavy drug doses he had taken the night before.

He slept the afternoon away and finally prepared to head back to his den that he shared with Keith and John. His dad walked with him to his car. Before Bill sat behind the steering wheel dad put his hand on Bill's shoulder and said, "Son, there are a few things I want to say to you. I don't know if you have been following the events in Iran where our boys are being held hostage. It is like a time bomb ready to detonate. The Super

Powers are posturing against each other, and there is the potential for global conflict. The way things are shaping up I feel that the prophecies of the Bible are being fulfilled and Jesus Christ could return at any time."

Tears trickled down Dr. Stafford's cheeks as he looked into Bill's sunken red eyes, "If Jesus comes back and you are not in heaven with me I think heaven will not be heaven without you."

Bill felt awkward and remained speechless. Silence prevailed. He had never lost his respect for his nom and dad and was aware that they loved him greatly. It hurt him to know he was breaking their hearts, but he felt incompetent to do anything about it.

Mom joined father and hugged Bill tightly. "We love you Bill and are praying for you."

Tears filled Bill's eyes, and rather than wait around, he kissed his mom, climbed into his car and drove off down the lane with his dad's words still ringing in his ears. Dr. & Mrs. Stafford watched with moistened cheeks until the car disappeared from their view.

"Honey, I wonder if we will ever see Bill in heaven?" yearned Sue Stafford to her husband.

"We will," answered Dr. Stafford reassuringly.

Clouds of dust kicked up into the air in the tracks of Bill's car as he sped down the half-mile lane from the house to the highway. Before he reached the road he was already rolling up another joint to smoke. His dad's words had stung him deeply. He tried to forget them as he raced along the road towards town dragging on the joint of pot which was fixed firmly between his lips. Try as he might Bill could not put the sound of his dad's broken voice out of his head, and for the first time in years he felt smitten with conviction in his heart.

The hot and misty days of summer passed without any more conversation about spiritual matters or the imminent return of Jesus Christ when Bill visited his parents' home. However the seeds of what his dad had said still would not go away. That conversation, combined with his growing dissatisfaction and frustration with drugs, gradually brought Bill to the conclusion that he had to take some steps to try to drag himself out of the quagmire of drugs and immoral living. He had lived in the night clubs of Chattanooga every night of every week for too many years. After the excessive binges that would last for days Bill faced the same old haunting emptiness that dominated his life. For nine years he had tried to fill that emptiness by saturating himself more and more with what was considered to be pleasure by the crowd with whom he hung out. That pleasure had finally begun to take a heavy toll on his mind and body. Bill felt his life was even more vacant than his empty pockets or the lonely room he faced each night.

Still withal, Bill continued to frequent all the clubs where his friends hung out. Nothing had changed in the surroundings or atmosphere. The guys still pushed drugs and engaged in the same carousing that Bill had enjoyed with them for years. However, for Bill something had changed. He just did not derive any more pleasure from these obsessions. Every night after he returned to his room he would lie awake wondering what was happening to him. Was his life falling apart?

Deep down Bill knew what his problem was. His Christian up-bringing had taught him that the Holy Spirit speaks deeply in a person's heart. He also knew his parents had been praying for his conversion, and he would find rest only when he finally repented and turned to Jesus Christ. Bill tried to fight against these thoughts but they persisted. He felt as though the hounds of heaven were right on his heels and there was no way he could escape.

In September 1980 Bill read in the local press that his dad was due to preach a revival at Temple Baptist Church in Chattanooga. Pastor T. D. Burgess was a good friend of the Staffords and had invited Dr. Stafford for a week of special revival and evangelistic meetings. Bill decided he would go and hear his father preach.

He abstained from taking any drugs that Sunday although he was apprehensive about going to church. Five years without having been to a place of worship had alienated Bill from what it would be like to go into a Baptist church again. Would they accept him as he was? What about the beard, the long hair and his hippie-like appearance? These were his outward expressions of rebellion.

Bill need not have worried. He walked through the church doors on Sunday evening and felt he was entering a different world. He was warmly greeted by several ushers who shook his hand and expressed how glad they were to see him. Bill was surprised that no one spoke to him about his appearance. The deacons at Temple Baptist knew that this young man needed more than a haircut. He obviously had problems in his heart. They were very glad to see a non church-goer come to their meeting and some recognized that this long-haired young man was the preacher's son.

Timidly Bill made his way into the church and sat beside his mother. Sue Stafford was taken aback to see her son sit down beside her. She wanted to hug him but felt it would not be appropriate in the middle of the church. Joy filled her heart and her silent prayers ascended to the Lord for his salvation.

When Dr. Stafford entered the pulpit on Sunday evening the church was almost full. During the congregational singing the preacher surveyed the congregation. He was almost overwhelmed when he recognize that the longhaired and somewhat disheveled young man sitting beside his wife was his own son Bill. Dr. Stafford later said, "To be truthful, when I saw Bill sitting beside Sue, his long blond hair and unusual appearance meant nothing. I saw a soul. I saw my son and the potential of what God could do in his life and the opportunity this meeting presented."

Dr. Stafford's heart flooded with joy. He knew that Bill would not be at church if something was not happening in his heart. On the platform he shared with Pastor Burgess that his wayward son was present in the meeting and asked him to pray.

When Dr. Stafford was invited to preach he gave no recognition to his son's presence. The evangelist had already felt constrained to preach on the story of the Rich Young Ruler from Mark 10. Now he knew why God had given him this message. He spoke out of a full heart as he tried to restrain tears.

The challenge of the gospel was presented to all without eye contact between the preacher and his son. It could not have been more appropriate. The parallels were many. The Rich Young Ruler not only came running to Jesus, in reality he was running away from the things that had failed to satisfy his craving heart. The preacher did not know that Bill was trying to free himself from his past life, and that was the reason he had come to church unannounced. The Savior not only loved the Rich Young Ruler, He offered him a new life, eternal life. That offer was extended to all, and Dr. Stafford spoke enthusiastically of the love of God and the new life in and through Jesus Christ.

Alas, the Rich Young Ruler refused to follow the Savior because he was a prisoner to the things that possessed him. Mark's Gospel records that sorrowfully the young man retreated from the Savior's presence. After Dr. Stafford had finished his sermon an invitation was given for people to accept Jesus Christ. Various people, young and old, some weeping, made their way to the front and were met by the preacher.

So intense was the conflict that raged in Bill's heart that he gripped the back of the pew in front of him so hard he was sure he had left deep imprints in the wood. He realized it was a battle of his will. He wanted to be free from the vices that trapped him, but he was not willing to let them go. He was unwilling to pay the price and sever his association with friends in the drug world.

The invitation was concluded and Bill headed out of the church as soon as the closing hymn was completed.

After Bill left Sue and her husband, shared with the friends who remained at the church that their son had been in the meeting. Dr. Stafford never forgot that night.

We wept freely as Sue and I held hands and sang Victory in Jesus. We praised God because we knew that God had prevailed in our son's life. We could finally see daylight after nine years of tunneling through tears, doubt, darkness and heart-breaking prayers. There was such a revival in our hearts. Even though Bill had not yet come to the Savior we had the assurance in our hearts that God was working. It was as if God had spoken to us, "This is it."

We felt we had been in darkness for so long, and finally the sun had just broken through in our lives. A burden had been lifted. We still didn't know when or if he would return to the revival meetings.

Bill and Sue returned home after the meeting, but they did not sleep very much that night. They had been through many sleepless nights before because of their prodigal son. However, this sleepless night was different. Whereas before they had lost their rest because of anxiety, now they were so excited in spirit sleep just would not come.

Bill also could not sleep that same night, but for different reasons. The deep spiritual struggle continued to dominate his mind and trouble his heart. He recollected,

It seemed as if the hounds of heaven were after me. God was so real that night. I almost felt I could reach out and touch Him. Hell also seemed so near. I realized I had wasted most of my life. I was destroying my body. I had wronged and hurt my parents and had grievously sinned against God. I remember weeping at the thought of me, a pastor's kid, dying and going to hell. I cried out for God to help me.

I wanted to be released from the things that were destroying me, but I was afraid. Would the guys down at the clubs think that going clean would mean I would squeal to the police? Bill Stafford was only a little fish in a big ocean of drug pushers and users, but I was afraid of the reaction of some guys. Eventually I drifted off into a fitful sleep just before dawn.

Next morning Bill set out for his usual morning drive to Siskin Steel Incorporated praying and reasoning things in his mind all the way. He resolved to abandon drugs whatever the price might be. At the factory he spoke to several Christians who on previous occasions he had ignored but now asked them to pray for him. They were elated to hear what was happening in his life.

At four o'clock that afternoon he finished work and returned to the apartment. Bill was a broken man. He went to his room and fell on his knees at the bedside. "I did not know whether I should pray or call mom and dad. I grabbed the phone. Mom answered. As soon as I heard her voice I blurted, 'Mom I want to get saved.'"

Quietly she replied, "Let me call your Dad."

Dr. Stafford climbed down from his tractor to take the call. "Daddy I'm at the end of my road," came the voice from the other end of the line.

"Son, I've heard that fifty times since you've been on this stuff. Are you in trouble again?" Dr. Stafford was firm in his answer, for he was aware his son knew how to play the church game. If he had killed a fatted calf every time he had heard Bill say he was at the end of his road, he would have had no cattle left on the farm.

"No Daddy, I'm not in any trouble. I just want to get saved." Bill sobbed uncontrollably down the phone. He continued. "Daddy if you ever heard me, please hear me now. If I don't get this settled I'm going to hell."

It was then that Dr. Bill knew his son was serious in his appeal and said, "Meet me at the church office at seven o'clock."

Dr. Bill did not even take the time to shower. He and Sue cleaned up and got into the truck to head to Temple Baptist

Church. During the thirty mile trip they thought they were floating on clouds. They sang, they cried, they prayed all the way to Chattanooga.

Meanwhile, Bill was still weeping when Keith came home. He glanced in at his friend without asking why the tears. Perhaps a little embarrassed, he withdrew and gave Bill space to be alone. Instead of hitting the bars and clubs that night Bill got cleaned up and headed to Rossville Boulevard to meet his Mom and Dad.

In a small room that opened on to the vestibule of the church, mom and dad were waiting for Bill. When he arrived Bill reaffirmed that he wanted to be saved. His Dad replied, "Well son, you know what you have to do. Let's pray."

With that the three of them knelt on the floor. Dr. Bill had his arm around his son and began to pray, "Lord, Bill has come to get saved. Don't let him get up off his knees Lord until he gets to the bottom of the garbage can. Make him face it Lord."

Bill buried his face in the carpet until he was prostrate and with deep sobs he began to pray. Dr. Stafford said, "I heard Bill cry unto God naming those awful sins, the depth of depravity, the hurt he had caused to so many people. He just poured it all out. After he prayed Bill jumped to his feet and said, 'I'm trusting Jesus.' At that moment his life was changed. The change was instantaneous, radical and genuine. Never again did Bill have a flash back to his old ways or addictions. It was a miracle."

When Bill finished praying there were hugs and tears all round. Bill and Sue Stafford were overwhelmed. In the meeting that followed there was no room for preaching. After the opening song Dr. Stafford broke the good news to the congregation that his son Bill had trusted Jesus Christ before the service. He asked Bill to join him on the platform at the front. It was an unusual sight for an Independent Baptist Church. Bill's long hair, beard, casual clothes and general appearance were a bit outlandish for a Baptist church. Dr. Stafford stood with his arm around his son's shoulder and said, "Tell the people what happened tonight son."

Trembling in front of the packed church, Bill spoke up, "I accepted Jesus Christ tonight. I want to thank my parents for not giving up on me." Tears of joy mingled with shouts of "Amen!" and "Hallelujah!" from all over the auditorium. Pastor Burgess, sitting behind the preacher, was more vocal than anyone else.

Dr. Stafford began to unburden his heart and told the congregation of their years of heartache and tearful praying while Bill was wasting his life on drugs. His voice was broken and he confessed that he and his wife had hardly any more tears left to shed.

When the final invitation was given for sinners to accept Jesus Christ many crowded to the mourner's bench in front of the platform. Hot tears of repentance flowed. Lives were dedicated to the Savior. Prayers were offered for other prodigals. It was like the opening of heaven's flood gates as blessings swept through the church during the remaining five days of the revival.

Bill drove back to his apartment. Mom and Dad were a little bit apprehensive how Bill would fare when he returned to his friends and to his old environment. Before retiring that night they prayed that the Lord would safeguard their boy from any people who might drag him back to his old life.

Keith was at home when Bill arrived. All the way home the new convert had prayed that God would help him to share with Keith and John what had happened in his life. Keith listened quietly as Bill spoke of the events of the previous few hours. He wished Bill well for his new life and withdrew to his own room without further comment.

Every night that week Bill attended the revival meetings. On the following Sunday night, the final meeting of the revival week, Bill with other new converts, was baptized and became a member of Temple Baptist Church. For Bill baptism was a gesture of burying the old life and beginning a new future with Jesus Christ.

Like most new converts Bill struggled to come to terms with the assurance that his sins were all forgiven. Night after night for three weeks he phoned his mom and dad to ask their forgiveness for how he had hurt them. Undoubtedly, Bill was trying to make up for all the heartache he had caused them. Finally, Dr. Stafford had to speak firmly and say, "Bill don't you ever call us to bring this up again. I can't even remember the things you are apologizing for. Your salvation has been so glorious that all the past has been wiped out. God has forgiven you and the blood of Jesus Christ has washed those sins away. You do not have to ask God to forgive you again for that which He has already forgiven."

Dr. Stafford confessed,

I could not believe the transformation in Bill's life after nine years doing drugs and several times over dosing. Sue and I interceded for Bill every day and all day. We were aware of the pressures and temptations to which he would be exposed, and so we would pray, "Lord protect Bill. Put an angel around him. Don't let anybody come near him who would tempt him." We just put a fence of prayer around our son and asked God that whatever it took God would do to defend him from evil. Not only was Bill getting right with God, but the Lord was taking us into fresh dimensions of prayer and intercession, and we were learning new things. Day after day we were encouraged to see Bill's joy and enthusiasm.

Bill was only a baby Christian but was happier than words could express. He later claimed that if he had been a cow, he could have "mooed" all day. He had finally been liberated from his past life and old habits. He still worked in the same job, was still living in the same apartment, but everything seemed new to him. Miraculously the Lord took all desires for liquor and drugs from his life. He had no desire to return to the old hangouts in

Chattanooga. Even on the night he returned to his apartment after his conversion he was able to ignore the drugs that were available at the house and retire to his room to read and pray. He had lost the appetite for drugs and had found a new hunger for the Word of God. Never again did Bill take another illegal drug.

He perhaps expressed it best when he said, "After my conversion I really did not stop drinking. I just changed fountains. I am now drinking from the well of living water in Jesus Christ."

CHAPTER 7

IT IS NOT AN EASY ROAD

As a young man Bill discovered that oil and water are not compatible components. It was only after his conversion that he also discovered that it was impossible to remaining in the apartment while Keith and other friends still peddled and used drugs. However, he and Keith had signed a rental contract that neither could sustain alone. Even though they were both living in the same apartment their routine and interests were so different that they seldom saw each other. Bill was at church nearly every night, and Keith was still doing the clubs with other guys.

Back at the farmhouse and in Temple Baptist Church, family and friends were praying that the Lord would provide new living arrangements for Bill. The change came about in an amazing way. An old classmate of Keith's whom Bill had known but had not seen for some time, came to the apartment one day. He disclosed that he was having domestic problems and he and his wife by mutual consent, were about to split up. As a result he was looking for alternative accommodation. Bill shared with Keith and his friend that he also was looking for an opportunity to move out and perhaps this was an answer to two problems. They agreed to do a deal. The friend stayed over night and next day he picked up his belongings and moved in with Keith.

Bill was freed from his contract and a few days later he found a small apartment into which he transferred his few possessions.

The friends at Temple Baptist Church provided Bill with the friendship and fellowship he needed as a new convert withdrawing from such a wild life. They kept him busy and made sure there were few idle moments. The young man also accompanied his dad to various revival meetings.

In January 1981 he travelled to Fort Worth, Texas for a Bible Conference where Dr. Stafford was one of the principal preachers. During the conference Bill was invited to share his testimony. He was still a rough diamond. Although he was free from drugs he still wrestled with some idiosyncrasies and habits that nine years of drugs had engrained into his life. With plain and non-religious language he related the dramatic and miraculous transformation which had taken place in his life. The impact on the meeting was stunning.

As a result of that conference Bill was invited to join the Rick Scarborough Ministries as a youth evangelist. For six months he gained experience in evangelistic crusades in the southern states. However, his involvement in this evangelistic activity made him increasingly aware of his need for more consolidated Bible training. Having left high school without following on to college, Bill had no academic credentials. For five years his mind had been parked in neutral without any further educational training. Dr. Stafford strongly urged Bill to apply to the Criswell College for Biblical Studies in Dallas, Texas.

Under the careful tuition of Dr. Paige Patterson, Dr. Wells and Dr. Galliotta, Bill spent four years studying the Scriptures and growing in grace. These men and other faculty members poured their lives into Bill's. They realized he was a rough diamond who had not yet learned the "language of Zion." For four years they loved him, encouraged him and taught him until his grades began to improve and his Christian character began to be molded and matured.

Bill graduated from Criswell College for Biblical Studies with a Bachelor of Arts in Biblical Studies in May 1986. He was able to gain more valuable experience in evangelism as an associate with the Bill Stafford Ministries. For two years he accompanied his dad all over the United States and was responsible for organizing prayer support groups for Dr. Stafford's conference and evangelistic ministry. This was another learning process for Bill. He also had many opportunities to share his testimony at various conferences. Emerging out of his association with his dad Bill developed his own ministry in conducting youth camps, revivals and Bible Conferences.

It was at one of these camps that Bill met Judy Lynn Hailey. For twenty years the Milldale Bible Conference, near Zachary, Louisiana, had been an annual engagement for Dr. Stafford on the Labor Day Weekend. When Bill was a young lad he was a regular visitor at the camp.

In September 1987 the "Calvary Singers" were invited to provide music for the conference. On the first night of the meetings Bill sat at the end of a bench that was already over-crowded. It was only when he tried to make room for himself that he realized that the young lady he had crushed in beside was the youngest of the "Calvary Singers." After some jocular conversation about the lack of comfort on the bench he introduced himself to Judy Lynn.

At the meetings the next day Bill and Judy sat beside each other on less crowded benches and exchanged information about their mutual interests. They had much in common. Judy also came from a Christian home and her dad, Lawrence Hailey, was an effective evangelist too. Before the Labor Day Weekend had finished both Bill and Judy Lynn Haily were unmistakably bitten by the love bug. Four months later they were married in Jena, Louisiana in December 1987.

Together they were a competent team, and God blessed the young couple as invitations for ministry in various cities flowed in. Besides preaching the Word of God Bill shared his testimony everywhere he travelled. Judy sang at all his meetings. Many people, both young and old, were converted and led to faith in Jesus Christ. Further blessings came to their home in Chattanooga with the gift of two beautiful daughters, Starla Suzanne and Trisha Lynn.

Bill Stafford was a miracle. He had come a long way from the wasted years of drug addiction to the rewarding ministry the Lord had given to him. However, Bill needed a few other miracles for that ministry to continue.

When Dr. Ron Dunn preached at a Bible Conference in Woodland Park Baptist Church, Chattanooga, God challenged Bill to a full surrender of his life to Jesus Christ. Dr. Dunn stressed that the Christian life was more than difficult. It is impossible. Only Christ can live that life through Christians who abandon themselves to Him. Bill responded to the invitation. On his knees he earnestly prayed, "Lord, whatever you have to do with me I want you to make me what you want me to be."

God answered that prayer in a most unexpected way. At that time Bill was a healthy and robust young father of two children and busy in evangelistic work in spite of his past life. He enjoyed jogging and followed a good physical routine. Judy was at his side in the ministry God had given to him. His two little girls were his great delight. Life could not have been better. It was just when it seemed Bill and Judy had reached the peak of their happiness that disaster struck.

While mowing the grass at his home one day Bill experienced a strange sensation of energy draining from his body. He got frightened when his hands became numb. Even though he rested for a few days he still felt lethargic and drained. He had to force himself to travel long distances to fulfill his preaching engagements. Everything seemed a real drag. Consultation with the family doctor revealed that he suffered from Carpo Tunnel Syndrome which required an operation on his wrists. Bill wondered "Could this be the cause of the loss of energy?"

Following a slow recovery from the operation Bill still suffered from chronic fatigue, and he was recommended to take a month of complete rest. There were some outstanding preaching engagements which he endeavored to fulfill, but by the end of the day he was virtually crawling to his bedroom or to a nearby couch. This weariness which followed the least exertion, was accompanied with severe weight loss.

After almost a year of diminishing strength Bill and Judy became alarmed that he might be suffering from some malignancy. His bright complexion had turned ashen and pale. Bill's glazed eyes were sunken into dark sockets which were accentuated by protruding cheekbones and hollow cheeks. Even though it was obvious to family and friends that he was desperately ill, his frequent visits to the doctor failed to get to the bottom of what the problem might be. The accompanying frustration and emotional strain took its toll on Bill and his ministry. It broke his heart when he found it difficult to fulfill his preaching appointments and had to cancel some.

Following another visit to the doctor's office in December 1990 Bill was shocked to discover he had lost so much weight. He was convinced that his number was up and this was the beginning of death. All the way home he wept at the wheel of his car. Although it was Christmas and the family had gathered for a special meal Bill requested to be left alone at home. He had no appetite. While Judy and the children had a meal with the Stafford family Bill sank into his favorite chair and prayed earnestly. Heartbroken, he admitted to the Lord that he felt he was going to die and asked the Lord if this was the end of life for him. The only answers that came were Bible promises that reassured him that God was in control and He had a purpose in all this mysterious suffering.

> The sorrows of death compassed me, and the pains of hell gat hold upon me: I found trouble and sorrow. Then called I upon the name of the LORD; "O LORD, I beseech thee, deliver my soul."
>
> Gracious is the LORD, and righteous; yea, our God is merciful. The LORD preserveth the simple: I was brought low, and he helped me. Return unto thy rest, O my soul; for the LORD hath dealt bountifully with thee. For thou hast delivered my soul from death, mine eyes from tears, and my feet from falling. I will walk before the LORD in the land of the living. (Psalm 116:3-9)

I shall not die, but live, and declare the works of the LORD. The LORD hath chastened me sore: but he hath not given me over unto death. (Psalm 118:17,18)

It was only in April 1991 after Bill collapsed in Birmingham, Alabama, that he was taken to another doctor, Dr. Roger Jones, who attended Bill's home church in Chattanooga. He recommended that Bill have an M. R. I. fearing he might have a brain tumor. This test revealed that Bill had a tumor on his pituitary gland. The tumor had upset Bill's whole chemical and hormone balance in his body. It was obvious that he needed major neurological surgery urgently.

This was a very anxious time for Bill and Judy. They clung to the promises that God had given to them. Prayer was requested all over the country.

Two weeks after the diagnosis Bill was admitted into hospital for the major and delicate operation. He was fearful and apprehensive. From the hospital he called his friend Skeet May, a godly member on the International Congress for Revival Board. He shared his anxieties with Skeet. His friend reminded Bill that the promises that God had given to him and Judy were just as firm on the day of the surgery as they were on the day they had claimed them. He must trust God's promise.

Before Bill was wheeled to the surgery room he knelt at his bedside and prayed for a miracle. As he drifted into unconsciousness under the anaesthetic Bill knew he was steadfastly leaning on the promises God had given him.

During the exploratory surgery the surgeon was able to locate and remove part of the tumor which was one inch in diameter. However, in removing part of tumor he was obliged to also cut away most of the vital gland.

Bill and Judy were greatly traumatized by the enormity of the ordeal. For two days after the operation dark clouds hung over the hills around Chattanooga, the sun did not shine on the city and it rained constantly. The dull weather only reflected the dark and somber mood Bill and Judy passed through as they anxiously waited to learn if the tumor was malignant or benign.

The first rays of encouragement came when Bill was able to surface in the ICU. He discovered that other patients near him were in a far worse plight than he was. Across the room a man lay flat on his back. He had a seemingly innocuous fall in his apartment but as a result he was totally paralyzed. In the bed next to Bill's lay a young man of nineteen who was justifiably distressed. He had mistakenly dived into shallow water and struck his head on submerged concrete. The accident had left the young man a quadriplegic. These severe disabilities of his fellow patients prompted Bill to thank the Lord that he was not paralyzed. It seemed as if the Lord was saying, "Bill, you are not suffering what they are suffering. I am only answering the prayer you prayed. I'm working in you to make you what I want you to be."

After a week in the ICU Bill was able to return home even though he had to remain lying on his back for several weeks. Before his release from hospital the surgeon was able to give Bill and Judy some good news; tests revealed that the tumor was benign. However, this news was tempered by the report that the surgeon was not able to remove all of the tumor and Bill therefore needed to attend the clinic for radiation treatment for five days each week during the following five weeks.

The whole experience left Bill absolutely spent physically, but he was glad to be alive and to know he was being treated. He underwent intensive rehabilitation therapy for a prolonged period. He was also prescribed adrenaline and hormonal supplements which he has to take for the rest of his life to compensate for the damaged pituitary gland.

It was during this enforced rest that Bill had plenty of time to think about his whole life. Not only were all his meetings cancelled for one year, no one was even inviting Bill for revivals. Furthermore, although kind doctors had waved their professional fees, Bill still faced enormous medical bills from the hospital. How will we ever get on our feet again? Bill pondered.

He felt he was all washed up and told Judy he was finished with the ministry. There seemed to be no alternative. Each day he looked in the classified columns for possible jobs. At this very low point God finally broke through, and again it was through Ron Dunn's preaching from Job on the theme, "Will a man serve God for nothing?"

At the end of Dr. Dunn's penetrating message rays of light seemed to show Bill that God had a future for him. With many tears he again abandoned all of his life and ministry to the Lord. He recognized that just as his complete deliverance from drugs had been a miracle of God's grace, so also his ministry needed the same supernatural power of God. Bill relates,

> I realized God was not finished with me. Little by little over that prolonged time of physical and mental rehabilitation the Lord was rehabilitating me in another way. I felt my life and ministry were on a downward spiral. It seemed as if my phone lines were cut off. No one called to invite me for any preaching engagements. I could see no future. It was only when I got to the very bottom that I discovered that that was exactly where God wanted me to be—emptied of myself to be filled with Himself. I began to see that Jesus Christ not only died for me, I died with Him to myself. I feel it took those two years of heartache, uncertainty, agony and brokenness for God to make me what He wanted me to be, and He hasn't finished yet.

The patriarch Jacob was one of history's earliest prodigals. He ran away from home and for many years remained in a distant land, far from his father and from his family. Before he returned home he needed an encounter with God at the Brook Jabbok. That meeting with God turned in to a wrestling match.

God prevailed over Jacob's weakness and made him what God had always wanted him to be—"a prince with God."

Bill also thought he had been wrestling with God during his two years of illness. What he discovered was that it was not so much that he wrestled with God, it was more that God wrestled with him to make him aware of his own weakness and prepare him for the ministry that God had planned for him.

Corresponding with the time of Bill's illness and recuperation, Dr. Manley Beasley, the founder of the International Congress of Revival, died after a prolonged illness. Dr. Bill Stafford had always been a close associate of Dr. Beasley in the International Congress on Revival, and at Dr. Beasley's request Dr. Stafford assumed the leadership of the movement following the death of the great man.

Bill's emergence out of his convalescence allowed him to slowly start picking up the pieces as he worked alongside his Dad. Little by little he accepted more responsibility and began testifying and preaching. This opened a door for Bill into public ministry and soon other opportunities began to flow for service in the United States and abroad.

Back in the late fifties young Bill Stafford, like almost every other American child, learned to recite the famous nursery rhyme, "Humpty Dumpty sat on the Wall."

> Humpty Dumpty sat on the Wall.
> Humpty Dumpty had a great fall.
> All the King's horses and all the King's men
> Couldn't put Humpty together again.

Bill did not know that he would live through a Humpty Dumpty problem in his life. He was born into a Christian home with many privileges but in spite of the Christian influences he had fallen greatly! Neither he nor any human could gather up the pieces of his drug-wrecked life and put them back together. However, Bill found the answer. What the "king's soldiers" could not do in the church, the King Himself did. When human endeav-

or could not rescue Bill Stafford, the King of Glory stepped in with wonderful grace to transform and regenerate him completely.

Although Bill and Judy Stafford still live in Chattanooga with their two sweet daughters, Starla Suzanne and Trisha Lynn, they are members of Oakwood Baptist church in Chicamaga, Georgia and are greatly supported and encouraged by the ministry of Pastor Darrel Henry and the members of the church. Today they enjoy a full ministry in many countries through the ministry of the International Congress for Revival.

CHAPTER 8
PARENTS AND PRODIGALS

In an ideal world there would not be any prodigal sons or daughters or even prodigal parents. However, in the real world they abound. There are no perfect children and there are no perfect parents. Furthermore, raising children is no picnic. It is tough and there are no crash courses or easy fixes that can prepare parents for what must be the greatest assignment of their lives.

The Bible teaches that successful Christian parents are those who train up their children according to the principles given in the Scriptures. The aim must be to help construct the lives of our boys and girls so that they grow into responsible adults who will be able to know God through Christ, walk in His ways and serve Him in a perverse world.

Relationships in a Christian family should be based on a sort of relay. Christian parents receive the love of God through Christ and convey that same love to their children. Such a flow of true love and godly living will create in the children an appreciation of proper values. Sadly, the communication of that love and outworking of these values are sometimes impeded by hurdles that frustrate the intended objective.

When this happens the frustration is generally attributed to problems that arise during the early years of parenting the developing child. It would take a whole book to address the numerous obstacles parents and children encounter during these formative years.

Bill and Sue Stafford like many other honest parents, readily admit that looking back on the upbringing of their family they had their priorities turned around. Dr. Stafford recognized the difficulties of raising his children in the shadow of the church and the peculiar pressures that fall on a preacher's kids. However, he confesses that these problems were exacerbated to the neglect of

his family by his over commitment to a busy program at church
and travelling to preach in revivals all over the states.

He admits,

> I was a workaholic. I wrongly believed that the
> way to success and to please God was work, work
> and more work. I guess I thought I knew more about
> pastoring than parenting so I gave my time to the
> Lord's work, and my family got the leftovers. This
> was not always done by design. Many times I tried to
> set apart time for the kids and my wife only to have
> that time robbed by yet another call at our home or an
> urgent visit that had to be made to a hospital. I was on
> a treadmill of Christian activity and could not get off.

Our children were at church just about every
time the church doors were opened. But church can
never be a substitute for a Christian home and close
personal relationships. It was only when our son hit
the drug trail that we recognized certain things we
had failed to do.

Sue and I look back on those child raising days
and realize we made a lot of mistakes. When we saw
Bill sink deeper and deeper into drugs we found that
the most difficult thing to handle was our sense of
guilt and failure. We felt we had broken every rule in
the book. Of course, the Devil is an accuser, and he
was not slow to hit us at our weakest point and level
accusations which brought doubt and sense of defeat
to our lives.

We came to the place where we had to recognize
that we could not change the past. We were absolutely cast upon the Lord and learned that our sufficiency
does not depend on our behavior but our completeness
in Christ. God knew we were failures before we ever
had our first child. We therefore had to believe that

God in His mercy clears up our past mistakes and in His grace gives us what we don't deserve."

Hindsight is a great gift. Generally we are wiser after we make our mistakes. When Dr. Bill Stafford surveys his role as the father of a prodigal he makes the following observations in the hope that other parents may benefit from his experience.

Attend to the needs of your children long before they become teenagers. "Train up a child in the way he should go: and when he is old, he will not depart from it." (Proverbs 22:6) To "train up a child" has the suggestion of shaping that child the way a gardener would bend and shape a tender plant or a young tree. "When he is old" refers more to adolescence and youth than to old age. It is indeed wise counsel that teaches that shaping our children into the way they should go begins before they are born. Perhaps in raising children it is the parent who is being trained.

Be sure you maintain good relationships and reserve periods of quality time with your children. Love must be more than a word that is used. Live love. Demonstrate love. Be sure your children know that they are loved and that parents love each other. To cultivate these good relationships there needs to be a wise investment of family time.

Discipline is the tough side of love. Children don't become rebellious. All children are born rebels. At school they will learn to read and write and a host of other arts and sciences, but no one needs to teach a child how to sin. Disobedience comes naturally.

To discipline a child is to educate and a disciple is simply a learner. Discipline is not an isolated act. It is an on going life style which associates disobedience and insubordination with pain and punishment. The objective of corrective discipline is to teach the child obedience and respect for authority. Disciplinary measures should be commensurate with the extent of wrong-doing. Some one said, "To discipline your child you can take away his money and his privileges, but you should never take away your love for your child."

Solomon taught, "He that spareth his rod hateth his son: but he that loveth him chasteneth him betimes" (Proverbs 13:24) According to this proverb parents who refuse to discipline their children do not show true love. Love may be an easy word to pronounce, but it can be tough to demonstrate at difficult times.

Be attentive to your teenager's behavior. Adolescence is a pressure time. Teenagers undergo all sorts of social, psychological and physical changes. They may be trying to cope with self-esteem, new values, peer pressure and a host of other demands. Don't respond to your teenager's behavior without trying to understand the under-lying reasons for his actions.

Keep the lines of communication open. Never close the doors of communication with your son or daughter. It is too easy for a parent to limit contact with his children to lecture or nag them. It is better to speak responsibly with them than to lecture them. Make sure that mom and dad remain the twin towers of strength and love on whom the children can depend.

Hold on to the promises of God. Sue and I learned to praise God in the face of difficulties and to hold on to Him in prayer for Bill every day. The Lord loves our children even more than we do. Do not give up on your children even if things do get worse. God who gave us the children hears us when we pray for them.

God's timing is always perfect. There were many times when we wanted God to answer our prayers immediately but we discovered He makes all things beautiful in His time. You can prove this too.

Even though peas may be taken from the same pod, yet each pea is different and distinct. We found that all of our children were different. Like their parents, none of our children is perfect, but their diversity added richness to their lives and to ours. I admit that Bill's nine-year roller coaster escapade with drugs and the associated degradation caused us a lot of heartache, many sleepless nights and perhaps the loss of hair. But his conversion and subsequent involvement in Christian ministry added a lot of color and happiness to the years.

To God be the glory.

CHAPTER 9

REVIVAL IS COMING

B ill Stafford, a former prodigal son, is now a co-worker at his father's side in the work of the International Congress on Revival. As a Christian Bill soon discovered that even though his conversion was one of the greatest moments his life, conversion was not an end in itself. It was just the beginning. Looking back, Bill is glad for all that God has done with his past. However, he refuses to live in the past. God has a great future for all Christians here on earth as well as a place prepared in heaven.

The Christian has not been saved from only sin and dead works in the past, he is saved unto good works which God has planned and purposed for him in the future. To accomplish that purpose God will often allow the Christian to pass through contorted and torturous experiences which will ultimately work for the Christian's good and for the glory of God.

Most certainly Bill and Judy Stafford and their two young daughters passed through their days of pain and darkness. At times they found it difficult to understand the way in which God was leading them. However, through those same sufferings the young couple discovered that their own weakness and deep brokenness contributed to the abandoning of their own plans in surrender to God's plan and His good timing.

These painful lessons were necessary to make Bill and Judy suitable co-workers in the International Congress for Revival with its emphasis on brokenness, prayer and fully yielding to the life of Christ in us.

What is the International Congress on Revival? Dr. Bill Stafford offers the following:

A Word About Revival

One of the most familiar "revival verses" of the Bible is found in Psalm 85:6 "Wilt Thou not revive us again that thy people may rejoice in Thee." Since the word "revival" is not mentioned in the New Testament many tend to ignore the drastic need for a fresh awakening today. We frankly admit that it is almost impossible to tie down what revival really is. Perhaps it is best described in Bible language which speaks of "times of refreshing from the presence of the Lord." Periodically God chooses to send a breath of heaven on nations, communities and churches where there is a sudden awareness that God is moving in an unusual way. We call that revival.

In my years of ministry where I have seen heaven touch down on a community or on church body some things were very evident. First, there was a genuine sense of utter desperation because of my own cold heart and my lack of real concern. My own deadness and that of others around me brought deep brokenness and repentance which drove me on my face in prayer before Almighty God. Added to my own plight, I became increasingly aware of the helplessness of the lost and the increasing lawlessness of society which needed an invasion of God.

Secondly, I have discovered that out of that brokenness came a spontaneous flow of life and power where men and women gave themselves to praying, weeping, and witnessing because of the quickening power of the Holy Spirit.

Thirdly, in the meetings I have witnessed a notable outbreak of public pleas from broken saints calling out for mercy or sinners crying out to be saved. At times there has been unrestrained and unprompted praise with songs full of holy desires and expressions of adoration and love for Jesus. This praise usually results in an acute awareness of God's presence. Frequently there are confessions of sin and restitution where other believers have been hurt. Church members whose lives were stagnant, uncooperative and critical, cry out for forgiveness and cleansing. They become wondrously filled with the Spirit.

Sermons that once were dead suddenly come to life. Following the preaching of God's Word penitent sinners cry out to be saved. Sometimes there is a break in the tradition of sinners responding to the invitational hymn at the close of a service, and they freely come to the front of the church during the sermon or return to the church to be saved after the meeting.

Finally, in revival we have often experienced an abundance of Christ's sufficiency which took over from dead works of human promotions and plans. The church spontaneously exploded into action with dynamic witnessing, Christ honoring praise and worship, sacrificial giving and demonstrations of the life of Jesus pouring out like rivers of living water.

The History of International Congress on Revival

The ministry of the International Congress on Revival began in the late 1970s and early 80s through a vision and burden that God gave to Manley Beasley to reach Europe. I had worked with Manley for many years and knew that he had a heart for revival. With a real sense of mission God enabled Manley to set up the International Congress for Revival with the specific burden. Even though parts of Europe were dominated by the Soviet regime Manley planned to gather pastors from various European countries and bring them to a central European city where, through the ministry of God's Word and through His servants, they would be stirred to believe God for revival in Europe and a personal revival in their individual lives and ministry.

The organizing of these Congresses involved paying for the travel of the pastors from their various countries, providing accommodation and meals and arranging local transportation. Manley, along with Ron and Pat Owens, set up the first congress and carried it through each year until Manley died in 1990. Following the home calling of God's servant, Ron and Pat Owens carried on the organization of the Congress for one year and then decided to relinquish it someone else.

Just at that time I received a call suggesting that I pray about taking over the leadership of this ministry. When I asked God for guidance He unmistakably burned the ministry of the International Congress for Revival on my heart. Right from the outset I knew this was the will of God for me. It seemed almost so obvious that since I had worked alongside Manley for so many years that the Holy Spirit passed the leadership of this ministry to me.

Although I felt God had impressed my soul with the burden and vision for International Congress for Revival I immediately sought the counsel of my wife and other godly people who had also been involved with Manley Beasley for years. They all agreed that this is the way of God for the International Congress for Revival.

Ron and Pat Owens graciously showed their willingness to continue to help us for a year during the transition for our first Congress in Vienna, Austria, in 1992. After the first Congress meeting started in Vienna and right through until the final service of that week there was a real confirmation to all involved that we had heard from God. The peace of God flooded my heart with the blessed assurance that He had initiated this work. I saw that it was His work and not mine. To me this meant that He would support and sustain His own work.

The Purpose of International Congress on Revival
The primary purpose of the International Congress for Revival has always been the message of revival. I remember speaking to Brother Manley concerning the will of God for this Congress. He spoke about only one thing—revival. Again I was reminded by him before he died that we must stay on course for revival. I have no doubt that revival is still our total objective.

Through the gifts of generous American Christians whose hearts are in accord with our vision, the ministry continues to stay on course to touch pastors with the message of repentance, brokenness and holiness which can be produced only by the indwelling Christ. Christ is our life. He is our sufficiency for the journey, and we are fully adequate in His adequacy.

Since 1992 the ministry of the International Congress for Revival, which began in Europe, has now branched into South Africa, Australia and Ireland. Scotland and New Zealand are at the praying stage and we are waiting for a word from God to proceed about this matter. Zimbabwe is also one of our great burdens, and we hope that this country will soon be re-opened to us. Revival conferences were held in Zimbabwe for four consecutive years, but they were interrupted by the inner turmoil in that country.

Whatever the Holy Spirit guides our hearts to do we will obey so that we may see revival worldwide. Our conferences in Europe brings together pastors from Romania, Bulgaria, the Czech Republic, Slovakia, Hungary, Poland, Croatia, Serbia, Siberia, Moldova, Ukraine, Lithuania, Germany, Austria and many other countries. The impact that the Congress has made is astounding. Pastors and wives have been challenged to believe God for revival in their local congregations as well as their own country. Each person is challenged to believe God to make them channels through which "Rivers of Living Water" may flow to their communities. We have witnessed the Holy Spirit work through key people with brokenness accompanied by tears, compassion and faith. Our prayer is that these preachers may be used by God as instruments of revival in their countries.

Personal testimonies at each conference show how God touches the hearts of many pastors. These testimonies bring joy unspeakable and full of glory. The visitors organize prayer meetings seeking God for personal revival at all times of day and night. The unity and love for each other makes each Congress a special time of building up and encouraging each other in the Body of Christ. Only in eternity will we really know the real results of these Congresses around the world.

Since the Holy Spirit impressed on my heart that the ministry of International Congress for Revival was my responsibility, there came over me an awesome sense of inadequacy and inability. However, out of that same desperation came a fresh burden from God and vision for the future direction of this work. It was then I suddenly realized that the Lord was initiating in me His burden and His vision. I discovered that my work was to cooperate and participate with Him as He worked through me His ministry and His purpose for the International Congress for Revival.

It is my burden therefore, to meet with pastors from different nations for four or five days and share with them the message of revival which is simply Jesus being Himself in us here on earth. We seek to teach them how to live in personal revival through brokenness and holy-desperation so that the life of Jesus will flow out to a doomed society. These rivers of living waters come filling and flooding our souls and flow from us until the tide of sin and unrighteousness is turned around and righteousness and godliness prevail.

My heart cries out for the men of God to remember their calling and to preach and re-fire their hearts to be God's men for this hour of decline and increasing infidelity. We often hear it said, "As goes the Church so goes the world." I believe that somewhere and in someplace there is a man that God will use to call the nations of the world to repentance before Jesus comes again.

It is our prayer that through the ministry of International Congress for Revival God will use us to be instruments in reaching other men of God and prepare them for a great revival.

While I was writing these last few paragraphs a call came through from one of the young preachers I have been able to teach and mentor. He called to tell me of another young preacher for whom we have been praying. There had been rebellion by one of his church members and the young pastor had decided to quit the ministry. In the meantime the Spirit of God humbled the young man and broke him. Following this he returned to his church and preached a message on "The Sin of Pride." People were smitten with deep conviction of sin. Many came forward to the mourner's bench crying out to God for cleansing and forgiveness. The young preacher started a prayer meeting on Friday evening with no strings attached and did not set time to finish. Because of that prayer meeting the church is now experiencing a fresh outbreak of old time revival. Church members have made restitution to the pastor and with each other. Their giving has been spontaneous and generous. Souls are being saved in the Sunday services in the church and in other places during the week. Attendance at church grown so much that the work is now demanding that they have multiple services on the Lord's Day. People are not only hungry to listen to God's Word, they are anxious to be doers of the Word of God with obedience from the heart. Marvelous things are happening in our world.

Oh how I pray for God to do it again in other places and revive His people that we may rejoice only in Jesus. This is my heart-felt prayer and expectation for these days. We must have revival.